T0255205

Lecture Notes
in Business Information Processing   364

Series Editors

Wil van der Aalst
  RWTH Aachen University, Aachen, Germany
John Mylopoulos
  University of Trento, Trento, Italy
Michael Rosemann
  Queensland University of Technology, Brisbane, QLD, Australia
Michael J. Shaw
  University of Illinois, Urbana-Champaign, IL, USA
Clemens Szyperski
  Microsoft Research, Redmond, WA, USA

More information about this series at http://www.springer.com/series/7911

Rashina Hoda (Ed.)

Agile Processes
in Software Engineering
and Extreme Programming –
Workshops

XP 2019 Workshops
Montréal, QC, Canada, May 21–25, 2019
Proceedings

 **Springer** Open

Editor
Rashina Hoda (iD)
University of Auckland
Auckland, New Zealand

ISSN 1865-1348   ISSN 1865-1356 (electronic)
Lecture Notes in Business Information Processing
ISBN 978-3-030-30125-5   ISBN 978-3-030-30126-2 (eBook)
https://doi.org/10.1007/978-3-030-30126-2

© The Editor(s) (if applicable) and The Author(s) 2019. This book is an open access publication.
Open Access This book is licensed under the terms of the Creative Commons Attribution 4.0 International License (http://creativecommons.org/licenses/by/4.0/), which permits use, sharing, adaptation, distribution and reproduction in any medium or format, as long as you give appropriate credit to the original author(s) and the source, provide a link to the Creative Commons license and indicate if changes were made.
The images or other third party material in this book are included in the book's Creative Commons license, unless indicated otherwise in a credit line to the material. If material is not included in the book's Creative Commons license and your intended use is not permitted by statutory regulation or exceeds the permitted use, you will need to obtain permission directly from the copyright holder.
The use of general descriptive names, registered names, trademarks, service marks, etc. in this publication does not imply, even in the absence of a specific statement, that such names are exempt from the relevant protective laws and regulations and therefore free for general use.
The publisher, the authors and the editors are safe to assume that the advice and information in this book are believed to be true and accurate at the date of publication. Neither the publisher nor the authors or the editors give a warranty, expressed or implied, with respect to the material contained herein or for any errors or omissions that may have been made. The publisher remains neutral with regard to jurisdictional claims in published maps and institutional affiliations.

This Springer imprint is published by the registered company Springer Nature Switzerland AG
The registered company address is: Gewerbestrasse 11, 6330 Cham, Switzerland

Preface

This volume contains the research workshops and doctoral symposium, as well as panel summaries presented at XP 2019, the 20th International Conference on Agile Software Development, held during May 21–25, 2019, at the École de technologie supérieure in Montréal, Québec, Canada.

XP is the premier agile software development conference combining research and practice. Whether you were new to agile or a seasoned agile practitioner, XP 2019 provided an informal environment to network, share, and discover trends in agile for the next 20 years.

Research papers and talks submissions were invited for the three XP 2019 research workshops, namely, Agile Transformation, Autonomous Teams, and Large Scale Agile. The workshops attracted a variety of agile software development topics related to the respective workshops. These included papers and presentations based on empirical studies and those conducted in industrial settings relevant to both researchers and practitioners. Submissions in various stages of progress were encouraged to generate discussions at the workshops. The workshops were structured to include a combination of talks, including keynotes by researchers leading the field in the respective areas, a variety of research talks by new, emerging, and established researchers, and round-table discussion style sessions. Research agendas for the communities represented by the workshops were discussed, refined, and reported in the respective workshop summaries.

The research workshops and doctoral symposium provide a highly relevant, friendly, and interactive platform to share and discuss emerging and late breaking research findings. They represent smaller, close communities of passionate emerging and established researchers and a psychologically safe environment to provide and receive feedback.

The success of the XP 2019 research workshops and doctoral symposium was possible due to the contributions of the organizers, Program Committee members, authors, presenters, and general attendees. Last, but not least, I would like to express my sincere thanks to the XP conference Steering Committee and the Agile Alliance for their ongoing support.

Panels at XP 20NN have been consistently among the best attended and well-received conference sessions following the conference plenary keynotes. This year's topics included: Security and Privacy; The Impact of the Agile Manifesto on Culture, Education, and Software Practices; Business Agility – Agile's Next Frontier; and "Agile – The Next 20 Years:" In the past we have published panel abstracts with panellist bios and position statements prior to the conference – however these abstracts did not reflect what was discussed at the conference.

For XP 2019, we took a different approach. We prepared extended summaries of the panel discussions, which captured the panellists' initial reflections on the panel topic, the principal questions from the floor, and panellist discussion. These summary articles were forwarded to the panellists for review, and the reviewed summaries have been included in these post-conference proceedings. We hope that you find this content useful and relevant to both software research and industrial practice.

Special thanks go to Dennis Mancl for his diligence in capturing and editing the panel conversations, the panellists for their participation and content review, and to the XP 2019 panel audiences for their questions and comments.

May 2019   Rashina Hoda
                                                                 Steven Fraser

Organization

Conference Chair

François Coallier   École de technologie supérieure, Canada

Research Workshops Chair

Rashina Hoda   The University of Auckland, New Zealand

Agile Transformation Workshop Co-organizers

Leonor Barroca   The Open University, UK
Torgeir Dingsøyr   SINTEF, Norway
Marius Mikalsen   SINTEF, Norway

Autonomous Teams Workshop Co-organizers

Nils Brede Moe   SINTEF, Norway
Viktoria Stray   University of Oslo, SINTEF, Norway

Large Scale Agile Workshop Organizer

Julian Bass   University of Salford, UK

Educator Symposium Co-chairs

Craig Anslow   Victoria University of Wellington, New Zealand
Martin Kropp   Fachhochschule Nordwestschweiz, Switzerland

Panels Chair

Steven Fraser   Innoxec Innovation, USA

Doctoral Symposium Co-chairs

Casper Lassenius   Aalto University, Finland
John Noll   University of East London, UK

Publication Chair

Philippe Kruchten   The University of British Columbia, Canada

Agile Transformation Workshop Program Committee

Finn Olav Bjørnson   Norwegian University of Science and Technology,
                              Norway
Peggy Gregory   University of Central Lancashire, UK
Tomas Gustavsson   Karlstad University, Sweden
Parastoo Mohaghegi   Norwegian Welfare Administration, Norway
Marius Mikalsen   SINTEF Digital, Norway
Teemu Karvonen   University of Oulu, Finland
Casper Lassenius   Alto University, Finland
                              Simula Research Laboratory, Norway
Helen Sharp   Open University, UK
Katie Taylor   Agile Business Consortium, UK

Autonomous Teams Workshop Program Committee

Antonio Martini   University of Oslo, Norway
Bjørnar Tessem   University of Bergen, Norway
Dag Sjøberg   University of Oslo, Norway
Darja Šmite   Blekinge Institute of Technology, Sweden
Gunnar Bergersen   University of Oslo, Norway
Jutta Eckstein   IT Communication, Germany
Maria Paasivaara   IT-University of Copenhagen, Denmark
Parastoo Mohagheghi   Norwegian Labour and Welfare Administration,
                              Norway
Marius Mikalsen   SINTEF, Norway
Rini Van Solingen   Delft University of Technology, The Netherlands
Thomas Gustavsson   Karlstads Business School, Sweden

Large-Scale Agile Workshop Program Committee

Steve Adolph   cPrime, Canada
Finn Olav Bjornson   NTNU, Norway
Torgeir Dingsøyr   SINTEF, Norway
Jutta Eckstein   IT Communication, Germany
Peggy Gregory   UCLAN, UK
Tomas Gustavsson   Karlstad University, Sweden
Andy Haxby   Competa, The Netherlands
Aymeric Hemon   Université de Nantes, France
Eric Knauss   Gothenburg University, Sweden
Maarit Laanti   Nitor Delta, Finland
Carl Marnewick   University of Johannesburg, South Africa
Nils Brede Moe   SINTEF, Norway
Helena Holmstrom Olsson   Malmö University, Sweden
Maria Paasivaara   Aalto University, Finland
Alexander Poth   Volkswagen, Germany

Ken Power   Cisco, Ireland
Klaas-Jan Stol   Lero, Ireland

Steering Committee

Juan Garbajosa (Chair)   Universidad Politécnica de Madrid, Spain
Ademar Aguiar   Universidade do Porto, Portugal
Hubert Baumeister   Technical University of Denmark, Denmark
Philip Brock   Agile Alliance, USA
François Coallier   École de technologie supérieure, Canada
Jutta Eckstein   Independent, Germany
Steven Fraser   Innoxec, USA
Casper Lassenius   Aalto University, Finland
Erik Lundh   IngenjörsGlädje, Sweden
Michele Marchesi   University of Cagliari, Italy
Maria Paasivaara   Aalto University, Finland
Seb Rose   Cucumber Limited, UK
Viktoria Stray   University of Oslo, SINTEF, Norway
Nils Wloka   Codecentric, Germany

Contents

Doctoral Symposium

Panels

First International Workshop on Agile Transformation

Agile Transformation: A Summary and Research Agenda from the First International Workshop

Leonor Barroca[1]([⊠]), Torgeir Dingsøyr[2], and Marius Mikalsen[2]

[1] The Open University, Milton Keynes, UK
leonor.barroca@open.ac.uk
[2] SINTEF, Trondheim, Norway

Abstract. Organisations are up-scaling their use of agile. Agile ways of working are used in larger projects and also in organisational units outside IT. This paper reports on the results of the first international workshop on agile transformation, which aimed to focus research on practice in a field which currently receives great attention. We report on participants' definitions of agile transformation, summaries of experiences from such transformations, and the challenges that require research attention.

Keywords: Agile · Transformation · Large-scale · Research agenda · Change management · Organisational change · Software engineering · Information systems

1 Introduction

In order to increase their ability to sense, respond and learn, organisations are up-scaling their use of agile. This implies that agile is used not only in larger projects and programs, but also in other organisational units outside of IT. In a foreword to the book "Unlocking Agility" [1], Bjarte Bogsnes writes: *The agile mindset is now finding its way into the C-suite, and it is starting to radically change the way organizations are led and managed. Business agility is on everybody's lips, for very good reasons*".

While the implementation of agile methods traditionally has been studied at team level [2, 3], adopting agile practices across the organisation is widening this perspective and has been labelled "agile transformation". Research has discussed three main areas of such transformations. First, challenges and success factors in the transformation process [4–10]; second, changes in roles and practices that occur during such transformations [11–13]; and third, models for understanding agile transformations [14, 15]. As an emerging research field, there are many understandings of what agile transformation is; also, current empirical studies tend to be descriptive and place little emphasis on theory to explain findings. This was the motivation to host the first international workshop on agile transformation in order to focus research on practice in a field which receives great attention.

This paper summarises the workshop, which was conducted in half a day at the *International Conference on Agile Software Development*, XP 2019. The goal of the workshop was to challenge the scientific community to identify what should be of prime

© The Author(s) 2019
R. Hoda (Ed.): XP 2019 Workshops, LNBIP 364, pp. 3–9, 2019.
https://doi.org/10.1007/978-3-030-30126-2_1

interest to researchers in the area of agile transformations, as there are growing opportunities to study them as companies increasingly adopt agile. Organisations are learning from agile practice to embrace agility in their ways of working; agile practitioners can also benefit from the wider context of organisations undergoing agile transformations, to understand their wider implications, and how to sustain them. The workshop received six submissions out of which four were selected for presentation. Maria Paasivaara was invited to give a keynote talk on tips for successful agile transformations. Following the presentations, participants offered definitions of agile transformation and discussed, in an open space format, the main research challenges in this area.

The remainder of this paper reports the results of the workshop, and is structured as follows. Section 2 presents the definitions of large-scale agile transformation from participants. Section 3 provides an outline of the four presentations and of the keynote. Section 4 provides an overview of key research challenges identified by the participants at the workshop and at a similar workshop in London. Section 5 concludes the paper.

2 What Is an Agile Transformation?

For many organisations moving towards business agility is challenging as there are many elements at play, from culture and leadership to process and tools. The participants in the workshop proposed different definitions for agile transformation as shown below; the terms 'culture', 'reactive/responsiveness to change' and 'continuous improvement' figured in several of them (Table 1).

Table 1. Some of the definitions of agile transformation gathered at the workshop.

"an individual's, team's, group's and organisation's journey into continuous improvements changing the way we do business, meet our goals and overcome our challenges by being more flexible, targeting smaller goals and providing continuous delivery, feedback and learning
the process which evolves an organisation to be more reactive to changes in its environment"
"digital transformation -> agile becomes larger (programs, portfolios) and more important; also becomes more complex, needs alignment with other units that are not traditionally agile; change in leadership and management"
"a people-centred approach to improving business outputs in the context of its environment the process undertaken to develop capabilities that will allow for flexibility in responding to a changing environment and continuous improvement"
"a path from adopting agile practices to establishing agile culture"
"transform from rather rigid structures, processes and hierarchy to a more network organisation with increased knowledge, understanding and collaboration across boundaries to improve a company's reaction to external change in order to improve performance referring to effectiveness"
"shift towards practices that enable organisational responsiveness"
"agile – iterative, incremental, collaborative, effects/results/outcomes-driven transformation – continuous improvement from where you are towards the Agile values and principles"

3 Experience with Agile Transformation

Lucas Green presented an industry case study of a big bang transformation with processes as usual having to coexist with new processes and resulting challenges; a research-based questionnaire was used to help understand team maturity during the transformation. A lesson from this case study is that the key to obtain understanding during the transformation is to support self-organising teams.

Akim Berkani discussed agile transformation beyond IT based on a case study of a French administration department. His approach took a management innovation implementation lens (new structures, practices and processes) to explain the transformation process.

Johannes Berglind, Ludvig Lindlöf, Lars Trygg and Rashina Hoda presented a study of an agile transformation in the automotive industry; their study was conducted bottom-up with the engineers who already practiced agile informally before the top-down transformation was carried out. They highlighted the paradox of top-down transformations not taking into account the informal agile practices already in place. They suggested an approach that takes into account these informal agile practices already present incorporating them into the transformation.

Katie Taylor took the lens of a practitioner business agility framework (www. agilebusiness.org) to identify the leadership elements needed for an agile transformation. She proposed the analogy of 'head, heart and hands' therefore focusing on people and their central role in agile transformation.

Maria Paasivaara gave the keynote at the workshop on tips for a successful agile transformation. They were based on past and ongoing studies of transformation processes in more than six private companies from sectors such as telecom and finance, and also from the public sector. The tips included ensuring management support, involving everyone in the organisation, communicating reasons for change, training everyone, hiring coaches with experience to help the transformation, ensuring transparency, developing an agile mindset, customising the transformation to fit organisation and product, including effort to improve, focusing on systems thinking as well as physical workspace and infrastructure.

4 Research Agenda on Main Challenges

We carried out a survey with the workshop participants; the same survey had been carried out with the participants of a similar workshop targeted at industry that took place in London, UK, two weeks before. The total of 39 respondents were distributed as shown in Fig. 1, with the majority having management positions (35%), followed by research scientists (29%) and agile coaches (18%). The 'Other' group was composed of

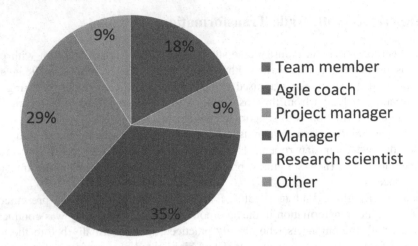

Fig. 1. Roles of participants at the workshops who completed the survey.

two consultants and one software architect. We do not claim that the respondents to this informal survey are in any way a representative sample of software companies or researchers in software engineering, but they are people interested enough in the topic to devote half a day to discuss it; they had an average of 6 years of experience with agile transformations (standard deviation: 6).

Participants ranked their motivation for agile transformation after a scale taken from the state of agile survey[1]; the top three reasons were: 'improve business/IT alignment', 'enhance ability to managing changing priorities' and 'accelerate software delivery'.

Participants were also asked to rank success factors and challenges slightly modified from [4], based on own knowledge of transformation projects. They ranked the top three success factors to be: 'changing organisational culture', 'leadership' and 'engaging people'.

Challenges were ranked as shown in Table 2. Participants could add 'Other' challenges to the list, which resulted in three more challenges: 'shareholder value dominates operating models', 'competence-building and empowerment of teams' and 'operations'. One respondent answered that the challenges available were 'not good'.

In both workshops, we discussed four of the main challenges and tried to identify relevant theory and research methods for future studies on these topics. More detailed minutes are available in a summary at the XP2019 programme website.

---

[1] See VersionOne state of agile report: https://www.stateofagile.com.

Table 2. Ranked challenges in Agile Transformations, challenges taken from [4].

	Challenge	Description
1	Hierarchical management and organizational boundaries	Middle managers' role in agile unclear Management in waterfall mode Keeping the old bureaucracy Internal silos kept
2	Integrating non-development functions	Other functions unwilling to change Challenges in adjusting to incremental delivery pace Challenges in adjusting product launch activities Rewarding model not teamwork centric
3	Resistance to change	General resistance to change Scepticism towards the new way of working Top down mandate creates resistance Management unwilling to change
4	Coordination challenges in multi-team environment	Interfacing between teams difficult Autonomous team model challenging Global distribution challenges Achieving technical consistency
5	Agile difficult to implement	Misunderstanding of agile concepts Lack of guidance from literature Agile customised poorly Reverting to old ways of working Excessive enthusiasm
6	Lack of investment	Lack of coaching Lack of training Too high workload Old commitments kept Challenges in rearranging physical work space
7	Different approaches emerge in a multi-team environment	Interpretation of agile differs between teams Using old and new approaches side by side
8	Quality assurance challenges	Accommodating non-functional testing Lack of automated testing Requirements ambiguity affects QA
9	Requirements engineering challenges	High-level requirements management largely missing in agile Requirement refinement challenging Creating and estimating user stories hard Gap between long and short term planning

5 Conclusion

This workshop showed that the research community is interested in continuing studies on agile transformations, and that there is a growing body of studies on which to build up. We hope the initial research agenda developed at the workshop will inspire future studies.

Acknowledgement. Thanks to all presenters and participants and to Rashina Hoda for chairing the research workshops. Further, we are very grateful to the program committee members: Finn Olav Bjørnson (Norwegian University of Science and Technology), Andreas Drechsler (Victoria University of Wellington, New Zealand), Peggy Gregory (University of Central Lancashire, United Kingdom), Lucas Gren (Volvo Cars, Sweden), Tomas Gustavsson (Karlstad University, Sweden), Teemu Karvonen (University of Oulu, Finland), Per Lenberg (Saab AB, Sweden), Will Menner (Johns Hopkins University, USA), Shannon Ewan (ICAgile, USA), Kai Spohrer (University of Mannheim, Germany), Helen Sharp (Open University, United Kingdom), Katie Taylor (Agile Business Consortium, United Kingdom), Marianne Worren (Norwegian Labour and Welfare Administration).

References

1. Hesselberg, J.: Unlocking Agility. Addison-Wesley Professional, Boston (2018)
2. Dingsøyr, T., Nerur, S., Balijepally, V., Moe, N.B.: A decade of agile methodologies: towards explaining agile software development. J. Syst. Softw. **85**(6), 1213–1221 (2012)
3. Hoda, R., Salleh, N., Grundy, J.: The rise and evolution of agile software development. IEEE Softw. **2018**(September/October), 58–63 (2018)
4. Dikert, K., Paasivaara, M., Lassenius, C.: Challenges and success factors for large-scale agile transformations: a systematic literature review. J. Syst. Softw. **119**, 87–108 (2016)
5. Korhonen, K.: Evaluating the impact of an agile transformation: a longitudinal case study in a distributed context. Softw. Qual. J. **21**(4), 599–624 (2013)
6. Peters, M., Britez, R. (eds.): Open Education and Education for Openness. Sense Publishers, Rotterdam (2008)
7. Paasivaara, M., Durasiewicz, S., Lassenius, C.: Distributed agile development: using Scrum in a large project. In: Proceedings of the 2008 3rd IEEE International Conference on Global Software Engineering, ICGSE 2008, pp. 87–95 (2008)
8. Paasivaara, M., Behm, B., Lassenius, C., Hallikainen, M.: Large-scale agile transformation at Ericsson: a case study. Empir. Softw. Eng. **23**(October), 2550–2596 (2018)
9. Kalenda, M., Hyna, P., Rossi, B.: Scaling agile in large organizations: practices, challenges, and success factors. J. Softw. Evol. Process **30**(October) (2018)
10. Kuusinen, K., Balakumar, V., Jepsen, S.C., Larsen, S.H.: A large agile organization on its journey towards DevOps. In: 44th Euromicro Conference on Software Engineering and Advanced Applications, pp. 60–63 (2018)
11. Abdelnour-Nocera, J., Sharp, H.: Adopting agile in a large organization: balancing the old with the new, Technical report 2007/12, Milton Keynes, UK (2007)
12. Jovanović, M., Mas, A., Mesquida, A.L., Lalić, B.: Transition of organizational roles in Agile transformation process: a grounded theory approach. J. Syst. Softw. **133**, 174–194 (2017)

13. Karvonen, T., Sharp, H., Barroca, L.: Enterprise agility: why is transformation so hard? In: Garbajosa, J., Wang, X., Aguiar, A. (eds.) XP 2018. LNBIP, vol. 314, pp. 131–145. Springer, Cham (2018). https://doi.org/10.1007/978-3-319-91602-6_9
14. Vlaanderen, K., van Stijn, P., Brinkkemper, S., van de Weerd, I.: Growing into agility: process implementation paths for scrum. In: Dieste, O., Jedlitschka, A., Juristo, N. (eds.) PROFES 2012. LNCS, vol. 7343, pp. 116–130. Springer, Heidelberg (2012). https://doi.org/10.1007/978-3-642-31063-8_10
15. Fuchs, C., Hess, T.: Becoming agile in the digital transformation : the process of a large-scale agile transformation. In: Thirty Ninth International Conference on Information Systems, pp. 1–17 (2018)

Open Access This chapter is licensed under the terms of the Creative Commons Attribution 4.0 International License (http://creativecommons.org/licenses/by/4.0/), which permits use, sharing, adaptation, distribution and reproduction in any medium or format, as long as you give appropriate credit to the original author(s) and the source, provide a link to the Creative Commons license and indicate if changes were made.

The images or other third party material in this chapter are included in the chapter's Creative Commons license, unless indicated otherwise in a credit line to the material. If material is not included in the chapter's Creative Commons license and your intended use is not permitted by statutory regulation or exceeds the permitted use, you will need to obtain permission directly from the copyright holder.

Second International Workshop on Autonomous Teams

Trends and Updated Research Agenda for Autonomous Agile Teams: A Summary of the Second International Workshop at XP2019

Nils Brede Moe[1(✉)], Viktoria Stray[1,2], and Rashina Hoda[3]

[1] SINTEF, Trondheim, Norway
nilsm@sintef.no
[2] University of Oslo, Oslo, Norway
stray@ifi.uio.no
[3] University of Auckland, Auckland, New Zealand
r.hoda@auckland.ac.nz

Abstract. To succeed in complex environments and handle the innovation, development and support, organizations have to find ways to support and regulate the autonomy of teams according to the environmental demands and limitations. Furthermore, there is no one-size-fits-all autonomy approach. The process of forming and implementing autonomous teams, as well as the effective functioning of such teams, is not yet adequately addressed and understood in the context of complex knowledge-intensive organizations. The second international workshop on autonomous teams investigated barriers for team autonomy: "What are the real-world problems to be solved for autonomous teams?" and "What concepts from the literature can be used to solve the problems?"

Keywords: Autonomous teams · Agile · Team design · Coordination · Self-managing teams · Self-organizing teams

1 Introduction

Digitalization is changing the competitive landscape in many industries. A company conducting a digital transformation needs to (1) cultivate the leadership for such transformation, (2) develop an agile and scalable platform on which digital product and services can be delivered, (3) design new digitally enabled customer experiences, and (4) incubate and accelerate emerging digital innovations [1]. Handling these four capabilities at the same time is a complex task on many levels in an organization. Teams designing new digitally-enabled customer experiences and incubating and accelerating emerging digital innovations are challenged by increasingly complex problems that also involve external actors. For example, a design or development team needs to interact with many experts outside of their team and department [2], needs to rely on a number of technologies and work processes, and frequently makes decisions with economic consequences. High productivity, innovation, accuracy of problem

© The Author(s) 2019
R. Hoda (Ed.): XP 2019 Workshops, LNBIP 364, pp. 13–19, 2019.
https://doi.org/10.1007/978-3-030-30126-2_2

solving, and fast decision-making are handled best by autonomous teams [3–6] (also known as self-organizing or self-managing teams).

Autonomous teams are described as teams given freedom by management [7] that take on the responsibilities of their supervisors [8], and are composed of people with a variety of skills to effectively tackle the variety in their external environments [9]. There is a high adoption rate of autonomous teams in many sectors, such as ICT, telecom, finance and banking, energy, transport and manufacturing. In the ICT industry, autonomous teams are exemplified by extensive uptake of agile methods [10–12].

The process of forming and implementing teams with high autonomy, as well as the effective functioning of such teams, is not yet adequately addressed and understood in the context of complex team-based, knowledge-intensive organizations [5]. Moreover, research on teams has predominantly been based on cross-sectional survey data, often involving student teams, and has not sufficiently taken into account the complexity in which teams operate [5]. We argue that more research is needed on roles, management, leadership, authority, decision-making, learning, technology, and the role of such teams in networks of autonomous teams. We know so far that the emergence of informal self-organizing roles facilitates the transitions in team practices and management approaches in the process of becoming agile [13].

1.1   Roles in Autonomous Teams

Traditional software development teams are comprised of formal functional roles such as developers, testers, and project managers. Agile methods (e.g., Scrum) replaced these with new formal roles (e.g., the Scrum master and product owner) that represent a cross-functional collection of old traditional (e.g. developers and testers), while also increasingly including other formal roles formerly beyond the core technical team boundary (e.g. the business analysts, user interface designers, and, more recently, artificial intelligence and machine learning experts).

While the composition of the software development team became more diverse and inclusive, these new and expanded formal roles alone do not form the basis of autonomous teams. What makes a software development team autonomous is the presence of temporary and spontaneously emerging informal roles, such as mentor, coordinator, translator, champion, promoter, and terminator [10]. These roles focus on: (1) mentoring the new agile team into agile ways of working and autonomy, (2) coordinating with the customer on a regular and detailed basis, (3) translating between the business language used by the customer and the technical language employed by the team, (4) championing the cause of agile and autonomous teams with senior management in case of bottom-up adoptions and championing agile transformation and autonomy with the teams in case of top-down adoptions, (5) promoting agility with the customer and educating the customer on his or her role and responsibility in supporting autonomous teams, and (6) terminating personnel not contributing positively to the agile ways of working and threatening the autonomous functioning of the team. Through the emergence of these roles, the team becomes self-organizing, with both the team and managers moving toward team-driven practices and empowering management approach respectively [13].

2 The Workshop and Papers Presented

The workshop included one keynote speech, "What makes your team self-organizing?" by Rashina Hoda from the University of Auckland. Further, the workshop had six presentations by researchers who had had their papers peer- reviewed. In a multiple-case study of three large organizations that implemented the Scaled Agile Framework (SAFe), Gustavsson [14] found that when several teams gather in joint events the teams get a better overview, higher feeling of autonomy, and the ability to stop planned work when it becomes too much. However, SAFe required the use of detailed plans and routines that somewhat reduced the team autonomy because the team members felt they had less mandate in choosing what to work on. In their study on large-scale agility in Bosch, Speigler et al. [15] found that low external autonomy limited team autonomy because of factors related to hierarchies, learning, structural dependencies, and rigid processes. They suggest companies need to foster learning organizations by providing time for communities of practice and open space meetings and tools to support transparency. Mikalsen et al. [16] relied on the Modern Sociotechnical Theory (MST) to understand team autonomy in a large, agile program with cross-functional BizDev teams. Their findings suggest organizations need to balance between agility and more standardized ways of working, and the de-bureaucratization ideal from MST is challenging to accomplish in complex organizations. Barriers for autonomy and efficiency included team members being dispersed, lack of team continuity, and use of shared resources. Petit [17] collected data, such as the quality of prior releases, to assess team autonomy from 70 teams in a bank. The teams were assessed using five levels of autonomy, and the effects of the assessment included teams governing each other as opposed to managers doing it, improved accountability of teams, reduction in time required for release approval, and reduced attempts to find workarounds and loopholes. Salameh and Bass [18] investigated how a large organization tailored agile practices to balance team autonomy and alignment. They reported on factors that promote the effectiveness of autonomous teams, such as informal and on-demand knowledge-sharing, collective code ownership, and the use of Lean Startup. Finally, Hukkelberg and Berntzen [19] reported on the challenges associated with integrating the data science role in agile autonomous teams, such as a lack of knowledge of the data science role (leading to sub-optimal use of the data scientist), the use of agile practices, and the lack of infrastructure. They suggested teams that want to expand with data scientist roles should arrange team kick-off, adjust their agile practices, use communities of practice, and provide training about the data science role and machine learning.

In addition to the paper presentation there were two interactive sessions. In the first session, we collected feedback on team size for autonomous teams and the barriers for such teams using Mentimeter (a tool for receiving feedback from the participants). The second session was a group discussion on the real-world problems to be solved for autonomous teams and concepts from the literature that can be used to solve the problems. These real-world problems motivated a discussion that led to a research agenda.

3   Barriers for Autonomous Teams

Mutual adjustment tends to be the primary coordination mechanism in autonomous teams. However, mutual adjustment in its pure form requires everyone to communicate with everyone. Therefore, the teams need to be dense, and since our communication abilities are limited that means they also have to be small. At the same time more and more teams are becoming BizDevOps teams (business, development, and operations in a team) to increase their authority, which often leads to large teams. We asked the workshop participants about the best team size for autonomous agile teams; 23% answered four to five members, 23% answered eight to nine members, and 54% answered six to seven members.

The actual performance of an autonomous agile team depends not only on the competence of the team itself in managing and executing its work but also on the organizational context. In the 2018 workshop, barriers were identified [12]. During the 2019 workshop, eight barriers for external autonomy were rated on a scale from 1 (not a barrier) to 10 (extreme barrier) (see Fig. 1).

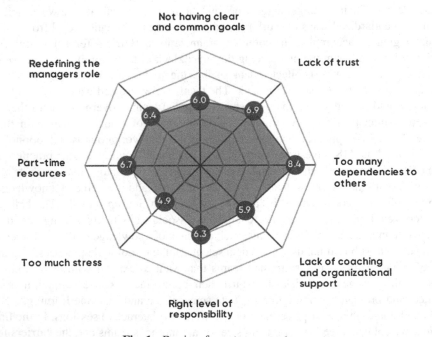

Fig. 1. Barriers for autonomous teams.

4   Research Agenda

Five areas of concern emerged at the workshop in 2018 [12] to help understand how companies can effectively enable autonomous agile teams: leadership, coordination, an organizational context supporting autonomy, design of autonomous agile teams, and internal team processes. Each area suggested research questions that can be used to identify factors that increase, moderate, or limit the level of team autonomy, and the effects of autonomy on team performance were suggested. In this year's workshop, the above-mentioned topics were prioritized. The rating was (1) coordination, (2) organizational context supporting autonomy, (3) leadership, (4) design of autonomous agile teams, and (5) internal team processes.

In the last part of the workshop, the real-world problems that need to be solved were discussed (Table 1). Concepts from the literature that can be used to study these problems were suggested (e.g., Modern Sociotechnical Theory, Coordination Theory, Actor Network Theory, and the General Theory of Software Engineering). When investigating problems related to the personality of team members, theories like Big five and Myers Briggs were suggested. Other suggested areas of concern were onboarding, shared mental models, sourcing, team, and multiteam systems.

Table 1. Real world problems to be solved.

Area of focus	Problem to be solved
Complexity and roles	Complex products and domains increase the need for large cross functional teams (e.g. BizDevOps). But smaller teams are more efficient than larger teams
Distributed teams	Distribution requires formation of virtual and remote teams. Creating virtual autonomous teams is a challenge. How to collaborate with outsourced teams
Inter-team coordination	Large projects and programs slow down the team. How can coordination be more efficient? How to balance the alignment of many teams vs. team autonomy?
Organizational structure	Autonomous teams need large networks but also work without too many interruptions. There is a problem building a network fast and maintaining the network and, at the same time, have time to do solve the team's tasks
Personality	Personality can impact communication, coordination, and decision-making. However, you often have limited influence on who is on the team. What personality types or attributes foster autonomy? How to handle individual vs. team autonomy?
Middle management and governance	Middle management need to support the teams and give the teams authority. What is the role of middle management, who decides what, and how do you balance management control vs. team autonomy? What legacy roles are needed?
Team membership	Stable teams is one key factor. However, teams grow and need new competence. Further, people want to change teams, projects and even companies. So how do you handle rotation and onboarding of new members?
Define and measure	The organization needs some control and feedback. However, the team should not collect data that is not used for the team to improve

5 Conclusion

This paper gives an overview of what practitioners and researchers in the field of agile software development believe are emergent research themes for autonomous teams. Top-rated barriers for autonomous teams were (1) too many dependencies on others, (2) lack of trust, and (3) part-time resources. Further top-rated research topics for future research are coordination, organizational context supporting autonomy, and leadership.

Acknowledgement. The Research Council of Norway partially supported this work through grant 267704. Additional support was provided by the following companies: Kantega, Knowit, Storebrand, and Sbanken. Thank you to the program committee members for thorough reviews and all the workshop participants for engaging discussions.

References

1. Sia, S.K., Soh, C., Weill, P.: How DBS bank pursued a digital business strategy. MIS Q. Executive **15**, 105–121 (2016)
2. Šmite, D., Moe, N.B., Šāblis, A., Wohlin, C.: Software teams and their knowledge networks in large-scale software development. Inf. Softw. Technol. **86**, 71–86 (2017)
3. Cohen, S.G., Bailey, D.E.: What makes teams work: group effectiveness research from the shop floor to the executive suite. J. Manag. **23**, 239–290 (1997)
4. Hoegl, M., Parboteeah, K.P.: Autonomy and teamwork in innovative projects. Hum. Resour. Manag. **45**, 67–79 (2006)
5. Mathieu, J., Maynard, M.T., Rapp, T., Gilson, L.: Team effectiveness 1997–2007: a review of recent advancements and a glimpse into the future. J. Manag. **34**, 410–476 (2008)
6. Hollenbeck, J.R., Beersma, B., Schouten, M.E.: Beyond team types and taxonomies: a dimensional scaling conceptualization for team description. Acad. Manag. Rev. **37**, 82–106 (2012)
7. Takeuchi, H., Nonaka, I.: The new product development game. Harv. Bus. Rev. **64**, 137–146 (1986)
8. Trist, E.: The evolution of socio-technical systems: a conceptual framework and an action research program. Ontario Quality of Working Life Centre (1981)
9. Morgan, G.: Images of Organizations. SAGE Publications, Thousand Oaks (2006)
10. Hoda, R., Noble, J., Marshall, S.: Self-organizing roles on agile software development teams. IEEE Trans. Softw. Eng. **39**, 422–444 (2013)
11. Dingsøyr, T., Nerur, S., Balijepally, V., Moe, N.B.: A decade of agile methodologies: towards explaining agile software development. J. Syst. SW **85**(6), 1213–1221 (2012)
12. Stray, V., Moe, N.B., Hoda, R.: Autonomous agile teams: challenges and future directions for research. In: Proceedings of the 19th International Conference on Agile Software Development: Companion, pp. 1–5. ACM, Porto (2018)
13. Hoda, R., Noble, J.: Becoming agile: a grounded theory of agile transitions in practice. In: Proceedings of the 39th International Conference on Software Engineering (2017)
14. Gustavsson, T.: Voices from the teams - impacts on autonomy in large-scale agile software development settings. In: Hoda, R. (ed.) XP 2019 Workshops. LNBIP, vol. 364, pp. 29–36. Springer, Cham (2019)

15. Spiegler, S.V., Heinecke, C., Wagner, S.: The influence of culture and structure on autonomous teams in established companies. In: Hoda, R. (ed.) XP 2019 Workshops. LNBIP, vol. 364, pp. 46–54. Springer, Cham (2019)
16. Mikalsen, M., Næsje, M., Reime, E.A., Solem, A.: Agile autonomous teams in complex organizations. In: Hoda, R. (ed.) XP 2019 Workshops. LNBIP, vol. 364, pp. 55–63. Springer, Cham (2019)
17. Petit, Y., Marnewick, C.: Earn your wings: a novel approach to deployment governance. In: Hoda, R. (ed.) XP 2019 Workshops. LNBIP, vol. 364, pp. 64–71. Springer, Cham (2019)
18. Salameh, A., Bass, J.M.: Spotify tailoring for promoting effectiveness in cross-functional autonomous squads. In: Hoda, R. (ed.) XP 2019 Workshops. LNBIP, vol. 364, pp. 20–28. Springer, Cham (2019)
19. Hukkelberg, I., Berntzen, M.: Exploring the challenges of integrating data science roles in agile autonomous teams. In: Hoda, R. (ed.) XP 2019 Workshops. LNBIP, vol. 364, pp. 37–45. Springer, Cham (2019)

Open Access This chapter is licensed under the terms of the Creative Commons Attribution 4.0 International License (http://creativecommons.org/licenses/by/4.0/), which permits use, sharing, adaptation, distribution and reproduction in any medium or format, as long as you give appropriate credit to the original author(s) and the source, provide a link to the Creative Commons license and indicate if changes were made.

The images or other third party material in this chapter are included in the chapter's Creative Commons license, unless indicated otherwise in a credit line to the material. If material is not included in the chapter's Creative Commons license and your intended use is not permitted by statutory regulation or exceeds the permitted use, you will need to obtain permission directly from the copyright holder.

Spotify Tailoring for Promoting Effectiveness in Cross-Functional Autonomous Squads

Abdallah Salameh$^{(\boxtimes)}$ ⓘ and Julian M. Bass ⓘ

University of Salford, 43 Crescent, Salford M5 4WT, UK
{a.salameh,j.bass}@salford.ac.uk

Abstract. Organisations tend to tailor agile methods to scale employed practices to have cross-functional autonomous teams while promoting sustainable creative and productive development at a constant pace. Thus, it is important to investigate how organisations tailor agile practices to get the balance right between teams' autonomy and alignment. Spotify model is originally introduced to facilitate the development of music streaming services in a very large-scale project with a Business-to-Consumer (B2C) model. However, developing a large-scale mission-critical project with a Business-to-Business (B2B) model is not essentially supported by the Spotify model. Thus, embracing Spotify model for such projects should be concerned about the question of *how Spotify practices are adjusted to promote effectiveness of cross-functional autonomous squads in a mission-critical project with B2B model?*

In this paper, we conduct a longitudinal embedded case study, which lasted 21 months during which 14 semi-structured interviews were conducted. The Grounded Theory (GT) is adopted to analyse the collected data. As a result, we identify practices and processes that promote effectiveness in cross-functional autonomous squads, which have never been discussed in terms of Spotify model before. We also present *"Spotify Tailoring"* by highlighting modified and newly introduced practices by the organisation in which the case study was conducted.

Keywords: Spotify · Tailoring · Autonomous teams ·
Cross-functional · Large-scale agile · Offshore · Outsource ·
Mission-critical · Case study

1 Introduction

The introduction of agile development has shifted the focus from the individual level into the team level by employing self-organising teams that are autonomous but aligned [5,8]. To succeed in complex environments, software organisations should find ways to build their teams' autonomy based on their environmental demands and limitations as there is no one size fits all autonomy approach [9]. In

© The Author(s) 2019
R. Hoda (Ed.): XP 2019 Workshops, LNBIP 364, pp. 20–28, 2019.
https://doi.org/10.1007/978-3-030-30126-2_3

fact, the topic of autonomous teams is immature within software engineering as there are challenges and future research directions that need to be addressed [9].

Spotify model is created around autonomous yet aligned squads [4]. It has been introduced for a very large-scale project with hundreds of developers over 40 teams across 4 cities [4]. Due to the lack of scientific research on this model, there were no guidelines about how to build and maintain the alignment between the squads. In our previous work [8], we determined the influential factors on aligning Spotify squads in a large-scale project. In this paper, we aim to find *how Spotify practices are adjusted to promote effectiveness of cross-functional autonomous squads in a mission-critical project with B2B model?*

We carry out a longitudinal embedded case study in a very large-scale organisation which has a large-scale offshore outsourced mission-critical software project. We conduct direct observation over 21 months and 14 semi-structured practitioner interviews to find out how organisations are actually tailoring agile practices to get the balance right between teams' autonomy and alignment.

We identify utilised practices and processes that promote effectiveness in cross-functional autonomous squads. This effectiveness is presented in the ability of aligning the Spotify squads which in turn enables squads' autonomy. To the best of our knowledge, these practices and processes have not been identified before in terms of Spotify model. Due to the confidentiality agreement with the organisation, we do not provide a detailed description of the explored project.

2   Spotify Model

Spotify model, which is driven by creating cross-functional autonomous squads, is a result of tailoring Scrum and Lean methods to fit a very-large scale project [4,8]. Spotify squads are encouraged to use Lean Startup, which promote innovation [4]. The overall structure consists of Squads, Chapters, Guilds and Tribes [4]. Squads have access to agile coaches who are in charge of improving squads' ways of working [4]. Also, each squad has a Product Owner (PO) who is responsible for (1) prioritising the work, (2) matching the product backlog, and (3) maintaining a high-level roadmap, which shows where the organisation is heading [4].

Squads' autonomy is presented in the ability for minimising dependencies among them, bypassing layers of management, and acting upon internal decisions without relying on other squads [4,8]. To enable effective autonomy, the squads shall be aligned together [4]. Spotify creates alignment by employing an adaptive structure, which is based on two dimensions, (1) vertical (i.e. Squads and Tribes) and (2) horizontal (i.e. Chapters and Guilds) [4]. Also, Spotify employs an *alignment on the product-level* to create expertise in specific areas [4]. In fact, previous research on Spotify model has identified influential factors on aligning Spotify squads by highlighting modified and newly introduced practices to the model [8]. This in turn indicates the necessity of expanding the alignment of the squads to cover further aspects based on the organisation's needs.

In Scrum of scrums, a synchronisation meeting is continuously conducted between the ambassadors of the teams to report completions, next steps and impediments [6]. However, having inter-team meetings with only participants of similar interests is considered more beneficial [6]. In Spotify, a "squad-of-squads" meeting is conducted in which the leaders communicate what problems needs to be solved and why. The squads are expected to collaborate with each other to find the best solution. Since squads share products instead of owning them [4], *collective code ownership* is adopted implicitly [8]. A synchronisation meeting is conducted on demand to coordinate the involved squads [4]. Facing conflicted priorities between squads demands inter-team coordination [8]. Tackling such tasks, which have conflicted priorities, by other squads who lack expertise on the product-level demands a utilisation of peer code review between squads [4].

Spotify adopts a *fail-friendly environment*, which is not about who's fault it is, but rather about capturing failures in a fast pace to learn and improve quickly [4]. Also, Spotify adopts *Postmortem Documentation* process, which is performed at the end of projects to determine what were successful or unsuccessful, to mitigate future risks [4]. Thereby, the organisation tends to *improve the process and the product* [4]. Furthermore, Spotify values *cross-pollination* more than standardisation as it causes less resistance.

The employed release strategy in Spotify is based on enabling *decoupled releases* that simplifies the release process and encourages squads to provide small and frequent independent releases [4]. To achieve this strategy, Spotify employs a *decoupled architecture* [4]. To expose possible integration problems and to minimise the need for code branching, squads are allowed to *release unfinished work as hidden* by utilising toggle switch [4]. Each client application in Spotify has a *release train* that departs on its regular schedule [4]. A *limited blast radius* process is utilised through the delivery of small releases over a limited number of end-users to do small experiments, prevent possible ripple effect, and to learn quickly instead of wasting time controlling all risks in advance [4].

3   Research Design and Methodology

Our case study is carried out in a very large-scale organisation that employs 650 staff members in 60 markets and processes around 60 billion EUR per year. The project, which is the scope of the case study, is considered as offshore outsourced mission-critical software project that manages autonomous financial services that operate under a common defined management policy. In this project, the development programme is of large-scale size [1] since developers are distributed over 6 squads. There are also 1 architect, 3 key account managers (KAMs), 5 POs (2 POs are empowered with KAM role), 2 agile coaches, and 1 test lead.

Due to the lack of scientific research related to the Spotify model, this research draws on a *longitudinal embedded case study* [7] to investigate how organisations tailor agile practices and processes to get the balance right between squads' autonomy and effective alignment among them. This research is comprised of *direct observation* of around 225 ceremonies that last 21 months, and 14 *semi-structured interviews*, which continued for around 50 min. After the second interview the questions were revised. Each interview was recorded and transcribed verbatim for detailed analysis in a continuous basis.

In this paper we employ the *GT* (Glasserian approach) to analyse the data. In essence, this is a process of continuous memoing, sorting, data collection, coding, analysis and constant comparison, and theoretical saturation. Open coding process is used to break down the data analytically and generate categories and concepts. While conducting open coding process, a few questions, suggested by Glaser [2], were asked to facilitate the coding process. A constant comparison was used to refine the categories emerging from the identified concepts. Furthermore, the observations were analysed and compared to the derived concepts from the analysed interviews. In result, minor contradictions were identified, which were explored and accommodated in the resulting grounded theory.

Table 1. Spotify Tailoring for promoting effectiveness

Category	Adopted practices or processes	Spotify	Case Study
Adaptive structure	Two dimensional structure	Yes	Yes
	Utilizing communities (Chapters and Squads)	Yes	Yes
	Utilizing communities (Guilds and Tribes)	Yes	No
Collective code ownership	Alignment over the product-level	Yes	Yes
	Adopting a reconciliation process	Unknown	Yes
Decision-making	Shared understanding of business objectives	≈Yes	Yes
	Emphasising on shared decision-making	≈Yes	Yes
	Utilising knowledge-based decision-making	Unknown	Yes
Inter-team coordination	Formal inter-team coordination	No	Yes
	On-demand inter-team coordination	Yes	Yes
	Informal inter-team coordination	Unknown	Yes
Knowledge sharing	Peer code review between two squads	Yes	Yes
	Limited Fail-friendly environment	No	Yes
	Routine-meetings for squad-of-squads and demos	Yes	Yes
	Chapter based knowledge sharing	Unknown	Yes
	Informal and on-demand knowledge sharing	No	Yes
	Postmortem Documentation	Yes	Yes
	Cross-pollination results in standardisation	Yes	Yes
Mission based planning	Innovation based missions embrace Lean Startup	≈Yes	Yes
	PL based missions embrace standardisation	No	Yes
Release strategy	Decoupled releases via decoupled architecture	Yes	Yes
	Unfinished work shall not be released as hidden	No	Yes
	Backward compatible releases	No	Yes
	Release trains (features with toggle switch)	Yes	Yes
	On-demand releases	Unknown	Yes
	Limited Blast Radius	Yes	Yes

≈**Yes**: partially covered, **Yes**: covered, **No**: not covered, **Unknown**: no evidence

4   Findings

In this section, we describe 3 emerged categories, which support the theory of balancing squads' autonomy and alignment to promote the effectiveness of autonomous squads, by describing only newly introduced and scaled practices. These practices, which are the main focus of this paper, are presented in grey in Table 1. The rest of practices and processes are highlighted on in Sect. 5.

4.1   Knowledge Sharing

Limited Fail-Friendly Environment. Spotify adopts a fail-friendly environment, which embraces fast failures to learn and improve quickly. However, the organisation in question utilises a limited fail-friendly environment as it provides mission-critical software service. *"As we provide software financial services, failure is not tolerated"*–P1, Agile Coach and Architect. However, failures are inevitable during the pilot launch of new features, which aims to improve and verify the behaviour of new features. When a failure is encountered, *"the responsible squad decides whether to switch off the targeted feature or to roll-back the release to overcome encountered issues"*–P7, PO and KAM. This in turn preserves squads' autonomy as only the responsible squad is involved in investigating the problem. Also, The organisation employs these introduced failures to embrace the learning and improvement for both of the process and the product. *"We share the reasons behind encountered release issues in our squad-of-squads weekly meeting to improve the product and the process if needed"*–P12, PO.

Chapter Based Knowledge Sharing. Spotify employs the communities of chapters, which represent the glue that sticks the whole organisation together, to establish cross-functional autonomous squads that are aligned together. In these chapters, members meet to help in solving problems within their competency areas. However, it is unknown if Spotify emphasises on the continuous sharing of knowledge within chapters. In the organisation in question, *"sessions are conducted to share knowledge and expertise within our chapters... At the end of each session, we plan for the next one"*–P8, Senior Developer. This in turn improves squads' abilities and strengthens their autonomy.

Informal and On-Demand Knowledge Sharing. While the software development programme in Spotify is of very-large scale (>300), the development programme in this organisation is of large-scale (<100). *"We do not benefit from Guilds and Tribes as the development programme size is smaller than Spotify's"*–P6, PO and KAM. Thus, guilds and tribes are not applicable for this project. Therefore, *"we call for meetings through Slack or email to discuss subjects of interest... Those who are interested can join"*–P10, PO. This in turn strengthens knowledge sharing while preserving squads' autonomy.

4.2   Mission Based Planning

The squads respond to customers' needs at different velocities based on their missions and scaled agile methods. While some missions value innovation more than plan fulfilment, others value plan fulfilment more than innovation.

Innovation Based Missions Embrace Lean Startup. Spotify encourages the utilisation of Lean Startup to promote innovation, likewise the organisation in question. Tasks of maintenance nature (i.e., adaptive or perfective) and/or of newly requested features are characterised with high degree of uncertainty. *"Developing new features and adapting or improving already existed ones impose challenges due to the high-level of uncertainty... providing dynamic and generic solutions increase the complexity"*–P9, Senior Developer. Such tasks require innovation to provide customers with business values. Hence, those squads tackling such tasks have missions that embrace Lean Startup principles. *"We have hybrid process based on Lean Startup and Kanban"*–P10, PO.

Software development estimation is considered as a waste. *"We sacrifice the predictability of delivery to provide valuable features"* P6, PO and KAM. However, *"customers request sometimes an estimation before starting the development... We provide a rough estimation and keep the them involved"*–P12, PO.

Product-Line (PL) Based Missions Embrace Automation and Standardisation (Plan Fulfilment). Since the project under study manages autonomous financial services, a PL architecture is utilised to streamline the process of integrating the project into external sub-systems. PL based missions embrace a "waste repellent culture" (aka Eliminating Waste in Lean Thinking). This is depicted through the utilisation of predefined checklists to automate software development. *"We employ checklists in our PL to speed up the process and to cover the activities of planning, estimation, documentation, code review, and knowledge sharing"*–P5, PO. This automation in turn strengthens squads' autonomy and alignment. PL related tasks are characterised with low degree of uncertainty since *"sufficient documentations are received to integrate to the targeted APIs"*–P2, Senior Developer. Since the uncertainty is low and the requirements are matured, a planning process is employed to predict the delivery. *"up-front planning and estimation processes are employed in our PL by utilising predefined checklists, bucket size, on-demand planning techniques, and Lead/cycle time"*–P5, PO. Hence, POs can communicate the delivery deadlines with the customers.

4.3   Release Strategy

Unfinished Work Shall Not Be Released as Hidden. Spotify releases hidden features that are not 100% done. However, the organisation in question does not release unfinished features despite providing all new features with toggle on/off switch, which allows either hiding or exposing new features. This is to make sure (1) having clean code base to prevent possible inconsistencies between the squads while collective code ownership is adopted, and (2) having stable features at production as the organisation provides a mission-critical services. *"It is crucial to have clean code base that only has stable working features as the code is shared by all squads"*–P1, Agile Coach and Architect.

Backward Compatible Releases. The organisation utilises configuration-driven development to control the behaviour of the software application, modules, or features at the execution time through configuration files. These files are used to (1) force certain business rules, (2) increase the software processing speed, (3) define interconnections between software components to make a compatibility, and (4) ease the development of correct distributed applications. Thus, the organisation provides backward compatible releases to prevent any deviation in the behaviour of the software service from the intended one in the old releases and to strengthen squads' autonomy. *"We always make sure that old features, components, and integrated APIs as well as their old configuration files working as expected... This is to satisfy customers' needs and to prevent possible conflicts of interests between the squads"*–P4, Senior Developer. Also, having backward compatible releases is powerful to facilitate the process of rolling back a release in case of encountering issues. *"New deployed releases shall be always backward compatible to be able to rollback in case of encountering issues"*–P8, Senior Developer.

On-Demand Releases. Since a decoupled architecture is employed in Spotify, a release train is established for each part of the software. Likewise for the organisation in question. *"We utilise a decoupled architecture to (1) facilitate the alignment of squads on the product-level, (2) mitigate possible dependencies between squads, and (3) prevent impacting the whole system when a mistake is introduced"*–P9, Senior Developer. However, it is unknown if Spotify facilitates providing on-demand releases in case of missing a release train. The organisation in question *"employs DevOps to automate the process of release delivery"*–P4, Agile Coach and Architect. Also, the organisation employs DevOps to facilitate on-demand releases in case of encountering a situation where a squad missed a release train. *"If we missed a release train this week, we can either wait for the next train or we can deliver the finished work whenever is demanded by a customer"*–P7, PO and KAM. This in turn increases the autonomy of the squads.

5   Discussion and Conclusion

To maximise success in software development, organisations tend to tailor agile methods to best fit their needs. One of the important reasons for the organisation under discussion to get transformed from Lean into the Spotify model is the need for loosely coupled, yet aligned squads while adopting different agile methods. Spotify has scaled agile software development to attain better performance, productivity and innovation [4]. Since squads' autonomy is a key driver to enable the aforementioned attributes [9], Spotify focuses on enabling autonomous squads [4]. In fact, a common ground through maximising customer value was found since the organisation was adopting Lean whilst the Spotify model encourages the implementation of Lean Startup, which promote innovation.

To investigate how organisations tailor agile practices to get the balance right between squads' autonomy and alignment, we conducted a longitudinal embedded case study in an offshore outsourced mission-critical project of large-scale. The case study lasted, so far, 21 months during which 14 semi-structured interviews were conducted. The GT was adopted to analyse the collected data.

Based on the analysis of the collected data, a synergy has been discovered between (1) the identified practices by this case study, and (2) promoting effectiveness in autonomous squads. This effectiveness is presented in the ability of establishing the right balance between squads' autonomy and alignment. Squads' autonomy and alignment are interdependent and can have an inverse relationship. Too much alignment might hinder squads' autonomy, but at the same time without alignment the squads can be autonomous yet not effective. Since self-organising teams are at the heart of Agile software development, teams must have common focus, mutual trust and respect, as well as accountability to organise themselves to meet new challenges [3].

Table 1 presents these practices and processes, which are classified into 7 categories. The first 4 categories in the table have been highlighted as influential factors on the alignment of Spotify squads [8]. These influential factors are only a subset of practices and processes that contributes to the effectiveness of autonomous squads. The last 3 categories in the table present the new emerged practices and processes, which are the main focus of this paper. Modified and newly introduced practices and processes are presented in grey in Table 1, which are discussed in Sect. 4, whereas the rest are already covered in the literature [4]. The table also indicates the coverage of the adopted practices and processes by the Spotify model and the organisation. Moreover, the table clarifies the extent of which Spotify model has been scaled in the organisation (i.e., *Spotify Tailoring*).

As for future work, we intend to determine employed product development practices in the context of scaled Spotify model for a global B2B model and investigate how these product development practices are correlated with the presented practices in Table 1.

References

1. Dingsøyr, T., Fægri, T.E., Itkonen, J.: What is large in large-scale? A taxonomy of scale for agile software development. In: Jedlitschka, A., Kuvaja, P., Kuhrmann, M., Männistö, T., Münch, J., Raatikainen, M. (eds.) PROFES 2014. LNCS, vol. 8892, pp. 273–276. Springer, Cham (2014). https://doi.org/10.1007/978-3-319-13835-0_20
2. Glaser, B.G.: Doing Grounded Theory: Issues and Discussions. Sociology Press, Mill Valley (1998)
3. Hoda, R., Noble, J., Marshall, S.: Organizing self-organizing teams. In: Proceedings of the 32nd ACM/IEEE International Conference on Software Engineering, ICSE 2010, vol. 1, pp. 285–294. ACM, New York (2010)
4. Linders, B.: Don't copy the spotify model, October 2016. https://www.infoq.com/news/2016/10/no-spotify-model
5. Moe, N.B., Dingsøyr, T., Dybå, T.: Overcoming barriers to self-management in software teams. IEEE Softw. **26**(6), 20–26 (2009)

6. Paasivaara, M., Lassenius, C., Heikkilä, V.T.: Inter-team coordination in large-scale globally distributed scrum: do scrum-of-scrums really work? In: Proceedings of the 2012 ACM-IEEE International Symposium on Empirical Software Engineering and Measurement, pp. 235–238, September 2012
7. Runeson, P., Höst, M.: Guidelines for conducting and reporting case study research in software engineering. Int. J. **14**(2), 131–164 (2009)
8. Salameh, A., Bass, J.: Influential factors of aligning spotify squads in mission-critical and offshore projects - a longitudinal embedded case study. In: Kuhrmann, M., et al. (eds.) PROFES 2018. LNCS, vol. 11271, pp. 199–215. Springer, Cham (2018). https://doi.org/10.1007/978-3-030-03673-7_15
9. Stray, V., Moe, N.B., Hoda, R.: Autonomous agile teams: challenges and future directions for research. In: Proceedings of the 19th International Conference on Agile Software Development: Companion, XP 2018, pp. 16:1–16:5. ACM, New York (2018)

Open Access This chapter is licensed under the terms of the Creative Commons Attribution 4.0 International License (http://creativecommons.org/licenses/by/4.0/), which permits use, sharing, adaptation, distribution and reproduction in any medium or format, as long as you give appropriate credit to the original author(s) and the source, provide a link to the Creative Commons license and indicate if changes were made.

The images or other third party material in this chapter are included in the chapter's Creative Commons license, unless indicated otherwise in a credit line to the material. If material is not included in the chapter's Creative Commons license and your intended use is not permitted by statutory regulation or exceeds the permitted use, you will need to obtain permission directly from the copyright holder.

Voices from the Teams - Impacts on Autonomy in Large-Scale Agile Software Development Settings

Tomas Gustavsson[✉]

Karlstad University, Karlstad, Sweden
tomas.gustavsson@kau.se

Abstract. Forming autonomous, self-organizing, cross-functional teams in software development is becoming more common even in larger organizations, and many organizations are implementing the Scaled Agile Framework. When autonomous teams need to work together, they must sacrifice some level of autonomy since work needs to be coordinated with other teams, which could be a threat to team performance. This study presents how perceived autonomy has changed by listening to the voices from the teams in three large organizations. Although several respondents did not express any experienced changes to autonomy at all, others put forth important changes. The practices where several teams gather in joint events are important arenas in both positive and negative aspects. The arenas give teams a better overview and a sense of being empowered in using their veto right to stop overload of planned work. However, more detailed planning in every single team could cause less ability to switch work between teams and a sense of suffocation due to detailed routines and practices.

Keywords: Autonomous teams · Self-organizing teams · Large-scale · Agile software development · Scaled Agile Framework

1 Introduction

Adopting agile ways of working and empowering autonomous, self-organizing teams in large-scale settings is becoming increasingly popular, and many organizations implement large-scale agile frameworks for software development [1]. When self-organizing teams need to work together, they must sacrifice some level of autonomy [2]. Design and programming need to be coordinated with other teams, and development efforts are often part of a portfolio or a program. According to Bass and Haxby [2], this means, for example, that self-organizing teams must sacrifice some creativity and autonomy to reach consensus on common standards. Reduced autonomy and creativity could lead to lower team performance, but the performance of an autonomous team does not only depend on the competence of the agile team itself; it also depends on the organizational context provided by management [3].

Also, most studies report positive impacts due to the empowerment of teams but some highlight potential challenges as difficulties in implementing autonomous teams

© The Author(s) 2019
R. Hoda (Ed.): XP 2019 Workshops, LNBIP 364, pp. 29–36, 2019.
https://doi.org/10.1007/978-3-030-30126-2_4

in certain settings or without sufficient leadership and support [4]. In the context of large-scale agile software development settings, there is a need for further research on the process of designing, supporting, and coaching autonomous agile teams to increase their performance. As highlighted in the proposed research agenda for autonomous teams at XP2018 [5], we need to get a better understanding of and deepen the knowledge about practices and strategies in forming autonomous teams. This will yield practical importance on how companies should organize for the right level of team autonomy and utilize autonomous agile teams in order to attain better performance, productivity, innovation, and value creation to strengthen competitiveness [5].

Some organizations, such as Ericsson [6], invent and tailor practices to scale up the agile ways of working while others implement full frameworks. The most commonly adopted framework today for large-scale agile ways of working is the Scaled Agile Framework (SAFe), according to the industrial survey The State of Agile [1]. Authors of SAFe, Leffingwell et al. [7], make a number of claims regarding expected benefits by implementing SAFe based on case studies written by end users. The highlighted benefits include, for example, increased team performance and more motivated employees. But these claimed benefits of SAFe do not stand unchallenged. For example, Schwaber [8], one of the originators of Scrum, criticize SAFe in several ways as being too top-down and inflexible, with the risk of suffocating teams under detailed routines and practices. This risk is verified by Conboy and Carroll [9] who investigated thirteen agile transformations and put forth that a major challenge was not to impose too many restrictions and rigidity when implementing a large-scale agile framework.

The purpose of this study is to increase our knowledge about team members perceptions from working according to SAFe; to understand how autonomy has changed since the implementation of the framework. The research question for this study is: *How is team autonomy affected by implementing the SAFe framework when agile software development is scaled up in the organization?* Instead of hearing opinions from method makers, let us hear the voices from the teams.

Three case organizations were investigated: Auto, a product development department within the Automotive industry. Gov, a project at a Government Agency in Sweden, and Bank, a development department in one of the four largest business banks in Sweden. The study of these case organizations began at the starting point of the implementation of SAFe, and interviews and observations went on for one and a half year. A survey was conducted about a year after the implementation began at the three organizations.

2   SAFe

SAFe consists of several roles, artifacts, practices, and routines described on different levels, starting from team level to the portfolio level, program level, and organizational level [10]. A very central practice is the joint planning two-day workshop with several teams for one Program Increment (PI) at a time, called PI planning. The practice, as described in SAFe [10], is aimed at dividing work and identifying dependencies between teams for a set period of time into the future; "PIs are typically 8–12 weeks long. The most common pattern for a PI is four development Iterations, followed by one Innovation and Planning (IP) Iteration" [10].

Besides PI-planning, there are other practices and routines such as Scrum of Scrums (SoS) where Scrum Masters from all teams frequently gather in short meetings to solve emerging dependency issues and System demo where several teams present results at the end of a sprint in a joint presentation event. As can be seen, practices and routines on the team level in SAFe propose several joint events between all teams working together. The artifacts, such as the Program board, are supporting tools to visualize the dependencies and the sequence of work.

3   Method

This is a multiple-case study where qualitative data is used to reveal how autonomy in teams is affected by implementing a large-scale agile framework. A survey was performed, and interviews were conducted. For further triangulation of data, several onsite visits were performed (see Table 1).

Table 1. Data sources.

Case	Survey responses	# of team members	Interviews	# of on-site visits	Hours of observation
Auto	109	80	9	6	196
Gov	56	39	4	5	113
Bank	36	31	5	6	70
Total:	**201**	**150**	**18**	**17**	**379**

The three studied organizations had implemented agile ways of working for three to five years with self-organized autonomous teams working side by side before they started investigating large-scale frameworks. All three organizations decided to adopt practices to be able to scale up and cooperate more efficiently between teams and started implementing SAFe during the beginning of 2017. Auto was first, starting in January while Gov began in March and Bank in April. The development organizations are divided into a number of teams with one Scrum Master (SM) per team and almost one Product Owner (PO) per team (some act as POs for two teams).

Auto is a product development department in an organization within the automotive industry which mainly develops software but to some extent hardware (20% of all development) as well. The observed department, when the survey was conducted, was organized in 24 cross-functional teams, divided into three different value streams or Agile Release Trains (ART) to use SAFe terminology [4]. The total amount of people working in the department was 141. The average age in the department was 36,9 years old, with an average of 9,5 years working at Auto.

The Gov-project is a SAFe implementation that started as a pilot project in a large Swedish Government Agency where large-scale agile processes were implemented with the aim of finding best practices to be used for the whole organization. Gov consists of seven teams working in one ART. The total amount of employees in this software development organization was 70 people. The average age at Gov was 44,9 years, with an average of 10,5 years working at Gov.

Bank is a department in one of the major business banks in Sweden consisting of seven teams that work together in one ART. They decided to implement large-scale agile practices because a new software platform was being developed, which would increase the number of dependencies between all teams in the department. The department consists of 7 teams with 42 team members. Bank is also organized as one ART in the same manner as Auto and Gov. The average age in the department was 38,9 years with an average of 9,6 years working at Bank.

Regarding the survey, paper-based questionnaires were used at all organizations. They were handed out and collected during planning workshops when all teams participated. The survey was conducted in February 2018 for Auto, in March 2018 for Gov and in April 2018 for Bank. The questionnaire consisted of multiple sections: (1) background (e.g., the number of years worked in the organization), (2) agile roles, team, and department, (3) opinions of working in a large-scale agile context and effects on teamwork. This study focus on Sects. 3 and 2 was used to identify which respondents who were team members. Section 3 consisted of a number of multi-choice questions targeting the different practices in SAFe (that will not be used in this study) and the following two open questions:

(1) "What do you consider as the main benefit of working according to SAFe in your organization?"
(2) "What do you consider as the main drawback of working according to SAFe in your organization?"

201 survey responses could be used: 109 from Auto, 56 from Gov and 36 from Bank, which represents a 79,4% (201/253) response rate. 150 of these responses came from team members (80 from Auto, 39 from Gov and 31 from Bank).

The open-ended answers were first inductively coded, and themes were created based on expressed benefits and drawbacks. Then, all responses were analyzed deductively, searching for opinions related to team autonomy specifically. These opinions related to team autonomy are used in this study.

To get a richer description, semi-structured interviews were conducted with 14 team members and 4 scrum masters. The interviews contained a number of questions regarding large-scale agile work, and one of them was the following specific question: In what way has autonomy changed in the teams since the implementation of SAFe?

Besides analyzing the answers from this question, the rest of the transcribed interviews were also read through in search of answers relating to team autonomy.

Also, a total of 17 on-site observations were conducted (379 h of observation) during PI planning workshops, from April 2017 until November 2018, a period of one and a half years. Besides the performed interviews and use of the questionnaire, these on-site visits gave an opportunity to informal discussions and listening in on presentations and meetings which all benefitted to a better understanding.

Thematic analysis, which is a qualitative inductive research approach [11], was conducted to analyze the transcribed interviews as well as the open-ended answers. The six-step analysis process [11] resulted in four major themes.

4   Results

From the answers to the open-ended question in the survey questionnaire regarding benefits of working according to SAFe, 23 were related to autonomy in teams. Two of these answers spoke of autonomy but were not part of any of the themes. Instead, they addressed the benefits of being autonomous: *"team autonomy gives motivation"*, and *"more fun and creative"*. The remaining 21 answers were grouped into the four major themes.

In 12 out of the 18 interviews conducted with 14 team members and 4 scrum masters the first, immediate, answer to the question: "In what way has autonomy changed in the teams since the implementation of SAFe?" was that it had not changed at all. But by going through the rest of the transcribed interviews, several answers regarding team autonomy could be identified. In the rest of this section, the four major themes based on both interview answers and open-ended questions, are presented.

4.1   Veto Power

An area where autonomy for the teams has improved, according to two of the respondents, is that it was easier to say no to more work now. Since the more detailed planning shows both available resources as well as "load" (the amount of estimated work each team has planned for), it was easy to see when there was too much of planned work. Both these respondents argued that, although this could have been done before the implementation of SAFe, it was easier now when everybody planned at the same time, in a joint workshop where differences between team loads became apparent.

From the open-ended questions, the answer *"it feels easier to reject/accept tasks"* also speaks of a sense of improved veto power for the team.

4.2   Give Help, Get Help

Another area highlighted by a respondent was that it had become easier to help other teams. The team member expressed that previously, when teams had a dependency with another team and the other team was delayed, they often just sat and waited. Now, because of the joint planning, the team knew more about the intended feature, and it was therefore easy (and fun) to walk over to the other team and help them.

The answer from the open-ended questions: *"problems and success is shared and highlighted"* shows that the single autonomous team are perceiving a heightened decision-making power in both giving, and getting, more help.

Likewise, five other answers to the open-ended questions put forth better possibilities for giving, and getting, help: *"better coordination between and within team"*, *"resource allocation is planned and reviewed/confirmed independently"*, *"includes everyone in the planning"*, *"visualization within the team"*, and *"we can see what the other people in the teams are doing"*.

Three answers related to improved competence, which makes it easier to help out, both within the team as well as other teams: *"Adds to a broadening of our competencies"*, *"Broader competence"* and *"broadening our expertise"*. Regarding competence to, four answers displayed the need for help because of the challenges in putting teams together: *"we are a team on paper but we can't have common goals since we have different distinct competencies", "to get the right people in the right places", "you are in a team where you don't have common tasks to solve", and "should have more mixed competencies in the teams".*

4.3   Less Choice of Work

Some respondents expressed the lack of freedom regarding choosing features to build for the team. Their explanation for this was the increased amount of planning, pre-planning, and refinement before each PI planning event. One of them, a scrum master, talked about the idea in SAFe that teams should be able to pick the features they want from the product backlog but that this was not possible in their organization. She reflected that it was not due to the specializations of the teams, but that pre-planning ahead of the PI planning event meant that product owners and stakeholders needed to discuss details with teams in advance and therefore, features naturally were dedicated to teams before PI planning. Another respondent viewed this development as something natural since, in his ART at Auto, they were now better at assigning larger features for each team, which resulted in better knowledge within a specific area. Hence, further development of features within this area was naturally assigned to this team. The respondent claimed that this probably was different in different teams since some had not as dedicated areas as his team had.

A related area, also expressed by several respondents was that requirements now, since the implementation of SAFe, were much more detailed in advance before the teams could see them.

> *"It is hard to really feel something for the features when they are already very well detailed when we receive them."* - Team member at Auto.

Two of the respondents saw this mainly as something negative, that the teams were not part of the detailing process. One respondent expressed a sense of "suffocation" because of less mandate in choosing what to work with. The third respondent was positive and meant that it helped the teams in understanding the requirements better.

Four answers from the open-ended questions also display increased managerial control and loss of mandate for decision making for the team: *"we still don't get to select features to develop", "too many managers/leaders compared to developers", "the teams are too much top-managed. They are better at sorting out problems on their own",* and finally *"it makes us work more like machines and less as humans".*

4.4   Speak up

One respondent expressed that there could be a downside to all joint activities implemented in SAFe with many people attending.

> *"If you are shy, SAFe is not any fun for you."* - Team member at Gov.

She mentioned the system demo, where she claimed to know people that didn't show all the details of a sprint result in fear of getting bad critique and be humiliated. She expressed this one step further by claiming that shy people will not like this way of working and that some colleagues once refused to present the teams PI plan in front of other teams. Instead, they sent presentation slides in advance but did not show up and later claimed they had missed the meeting since they did not know at what time presentations should start at.

Three answers from the open-ended questions expressed a loss of clarity due to problems with team members and stakeholders not speaking up: "*harder to get clear responsibilities, things end up between chairs*", "*unclear about who is in charge of problems that arise*", and "*lost sense of personal responsibility and urgency*".

5   Discussion

When self-organizing teams need to work together, they must sacrifice some level of autonomy. As exemplified by Bass and Haxby, this will have impacts on creativity and autonomy to reach consensus on common standards [2], but few details on changes to autonomy have been put forth in research on large-scale agile ways of working. Even less have been studied when scale-up is performed by implementing a framework, such as the increasingly popular SAFe [1].

Therefore, the following research question was formulated: "*How is team autonomy affected by implementing the SAFe framework when agile software development is scaled up in the organization?*". The multiple-case study conducted at the three case organizations Auto, Gov, and Bank, shows how the joint activities with several teams form important arenas that affect autonomy in the single team. The PI planning event, for example, creates a better overview which seems to allow better possibilities to help, and receive help, from other teams. According to the respondents, this also appears to broaden competencies in the team, allowing even more cross-functionality to the team. The increased planning transparency seems to empower teams, even giving them more veto power to stop poor resource planning with overloaded teams.

These arenas, however, do not seem to empower teams on their own. According to the interview respondents, they require people who dare to speak up, that are not shy or afraid to demonstrate plans proposed by the team in public. Respondents also reported a lost sense of personal responsibility and clarity regarding responsibility for solving emerging dependency issues. This further pinpoint the need for speaking up, to raise concerns, and clarify responsibilities.

Several agile practitioners, Schwaber [8] for example, have criticized SAFe for being too strict and formal, thereby risking to suffocate teams under detailed routines and practices. Conboy and Carroll [9] confirm the risk of imposing too many restrictions and rigidity when implementing large-scale frameworks from a study of thirteen agile transformations. This problem is somewhat supported in this study, especially regarding long-term planning routines. The "suffocation" expressed from team members relate to less mandate in choosing what to work with. Because of the added planning, pre-planning and refining routines, it seems as teams have lost much of their possibility to choose what to work with and to "feel" for the upcoming work, since much detailing has been conducted outside the team.

A conclusion from the large-scale agile transformation at Ericsson [6], who invented and tailored their own practices, was that they probably would have benefitted from implementing a common framework instead. They thought such a framework would have provided a common ground for team practices which could instead have been tailored later on [6]. Findings from this study, however, suggest that it is not that simple as having a shared framework. Implementing a framework such as SAFe could lead to other problems such as a "sense of suffocation" and less ability to choose between different features for the teams.

References

1. 12th Annual State of Agile™ Report. http://stateofagile.versionone.com
2. Bass, J.M., Haxby, A.: Tailoring product ownership in large-scale agile projects: managing scale, distance, and governance. IEEE Softw. **36**(2), 58–63 (2019)
3. Hoda, R., Noble, J.: Becoming agile: a grounded theory of agile transitions in practice. In: Proceedings of the 39th International Conference on Software Engineering, ICSE (2017)
4. Langfred, C.W.: Work-group design and autonomy: a field study of the interaction between task interdependence and group autonomy. Small Group Res. **31**(1), 54–70 (2000)
5. Stray, V., Moe, N.B., Hoda, R.: Autonomous agile teams: challenges and future directions for research. In: Proceedings of the 19th International Conference on Agile Software Development: Companion (XP 2018), Article no. 16, 5 p. ACM, New York (2018)
6. Paasivaara, M., Behm, B., Lassenius, C., Hallikainen, M.: Large-scale agile transformation at Ericsson: a case study. Empir. Softw. Eng. **23**(5), 2550–2596 (2018)
7. Leffingwell, D., Yakyama, A., Knaster, R., Jemilo, D., Oren, I.: SAFe Reference Guide: Scaled Agile Framework for Lean Software and Systems Engineering. Addison Wesley, Reading (2017)
8. Schwaber, K.: UnSAFe at any speed. kenschwaber.wordpress.com/2013/08/06/unsafe-at-any-speed/
9. Conboy, K., Carroll, N.: Implementing large-scale agile frameworks: challenges and recommendations. IEEE Softw. **36**, 44–50 (2019)
10. Scaled Agile Framework 4.6. www.scaledagileframework.org
11. Braun, V., Clarke, V.: Thematic analysis. In: Cooper, H. (ed.) APA Handbook of Research Methods in Psychology: Research Designs, vol. 2, pp. 57–71. American Psychological Association, Washington, DC (2012)

Open Access This chapter is licensed under the terms of the Creative Commons Attribution 4.0 International License (http://creativecommons.org/licenses/by/4.0/), which permits use, sharing, adaptation, distribution and reproduction in any medium or format, as long as you give appropriate credit to the original author(s) and the source, provide a link to the Creative Commons license and indicate if changes were made.

The images or other third party material in this chapter are included in the chapter's Creative Commons license, unless indicated otherwise in a credit line to the material. If material is not included in the chapter's Creative Commons license and your intended use is not permitted by statutory regulation or exceeds the permitted use, you will need to obtain permission directly from the copyright holder.

Exploring the Challenges of Integrating Data Science Roles in Agile Autonomous Teams

Ivar Hukkelberg[(✉)] and Marthe Berntzen

Department of Informatics, University of Oslo,
Gaustadalléen 23B, 0730 Oslo, Norway
{ivarhuk,marthenb}@ifi.uio.no

Abstract. The notion of autonomous teams is core to agile software development. However, autonomy in agile teams is challenged by increasingly complex software projects, large-scale agile and perhaps increasingly multidisciplinary teams. At the same time, data science roles are making their way into agile teams as companies seek to reap the potential advantages of using data to develop better and more competitive services and products. The consequences of implementing such roles in traditional agile teams are largely unknown. In this paper, we take an exploratory approach to the topic of data science roles in agile teams by a set of interviews with five data scientists as well as three members of an agile software development team. Based on the interviews we identify a set of challenges associated with incorporating the role in agile autonomous teams. Based on these challenges we discuss preliminary recommendations for companies seeking to integrate data science roles in agile teams.

Keywords: Data science · Agile · Software development · Teams · Autonomy

1 Introduction and Background

During the past decades, agile practices have spread beyond the traditional software development team to include other roles, parts of the organization, and even the organization as a whole [1]. This introduces challenges such as adapting agile methods while keeping with the central aspects of team autonomy and balancing cross-functional teams with an efficient team size [2]. At the same time, the usage of data science in software development has expanded rapidly [1, 3], possibly introducing new challenges to agile team autonomy.

The notion of team autonomy is not new. In most agile methods the notion of enabling teams to make decisions of their own is central [4]. Such teams are often labelled as self-managing, self-organizing or autonomous. These teams should be cross-functional, consisting of the roles needed for the team to utilize their competence to deliver across roles and organizational functions [5, 6]. The assumption is that cross-functionality contribute to more empowerment and participation within the team [5, 7].

Regardless of the label, merely assembling a group of people and naming them autonomous is not enough to ensure that the group acts as a self-organizing or autonomous team [7]. Some of the identified criteria important for team autonomy

© The Author(s) 2019
R. Hoda (Ed.): XP 2019 Workshops, LNBIP 364, pp. 37–45, 2019.
https://doi.org/10.1007/978-3-030-30126-2_5

include having a common goal and direction, a trusting team climate, organizational support and efficient skill utilization [4, 8].

The increasing scale and complexity of modern software development has led to new team constellations such as DevOps and BizDev teams [4], or more recently combining and adapting agile development practices to data science and machine learning [1]. Adding increasingly more roles to the agile, cross-functional team, may come with the side effect that autonomy and self-management is difficult to maintain [2, 4]. In particular, introducing new roles such as data scientists into the cross-functional team may pose a challenge with conflicting interest and needs across team members with different backgrounds, terminologies and approaches to work. Indeed, balancing individual and team autonomy are among the key barriers to self-management [7]. We speculate that including data science roles into agile cross-functional teams will further complicate the landscape.

1.1 Machine Learning in Organizations and the Need for Data Scientists

Today, extreme amount of data is generated and stored every day. Organizations are trying to use this data to create new experience and products that are personalized for its users and to stay ahead of competitors. Leading stars in this area like Google, Facebook and Amazon, have succeeded in creating value from the data they store. The key elements of their success lie in a strong digital platform where all data generated can be easily accessed. Machine learning, a subfield of artificial intelligence, is currently the preferred method to use in order to handle the extreme amount of data. Algorithms and statistical models search for patterns, make data-driven decisions and continuously improve themselves without human interference [9]. The people possessing the skill set to work with this combination of computer science and statistics are often referred to as data scientists. This role is not to be mixed with other similar roles, such as data engineer and data analyst. Data engineers are more concerned with maintaining and building infrastructure so that the data becomes accessible [10]. Data analyst build reports and visualizations to explain what insight the data is hiding using statistical methods, but do not spend time programming advanced algorithms that the data scientist role does [11]. Often, the data scientist role in an organization can be described as a researcher trying to find meaning in the data and creating self-improving algorithms [1, 12]. The solutions they build can lead to tasks automation, personalized user content, and much more.

Recently, more traditional organizations have begun to explore how to create value from data. Fleming et al. [13] point at different factors needed to build a data-driven organization. Among these, a key point is having the right competence, such as data scientists. However, merely hiring a data scientist and expect results is likely to be wishful thinking. According to Davenport [14], a good data-driven environment where data scientist can thrive should include a focus on (1) company culture, (2) analytics capabilities, (3) data and technology capabilities and (4) individual capabilities. Here we see that there are many factors involved in order to build a data-driven organization and incorporate the data scientist role. Patil [15] also points to the importance of close collaboration between data scientist and the rest of the organization, and that to create great data products you have to build cross-disciplinary groups. One can see this as an argument to incorporate the data scientist role into cross-functional teams. A data scientist also needs a work environment where he/she can experiment and let the creativity blossom [15]. This may indicate that they need a high degree of individual autonomy.

1.2 Research Question

While organizations are increasingly making use of both data science on the one hand, and agile methods on the other, little research has examined the interplay between the two, in particular from an agile team perspective. For instance, Larson and Chang [1] examine how agile principles can be adapted and adjusted to data science, but do not discuss how the introduction of data science roles affects autonomy in the agile team. Kim, Zimmermann, DeLine, and Begel [3] discuss the role of data scientists in software development teams, but not agile or team autonomy. As such, our knowledge about including data science roles in agile autonomous teams remains limited. In this study, we explore the following research question: *What challenges do agile autonomous teams face when introducing data scientist roles into the team?*

In this short paper, we take an exploratory approach to our research question. This first section has introduced the topics. Next, we describe our method and data collection procedures and present results from six interviews. Finally, we discuss the challenges identified from the results and suggest initial recommendations for practice.

2 Method

To explore our research question, we conducted six semi-structured interviews with an average length of 40 min. Five separate individual interviews with participants from three different organizations were conducted by the first author. The second author held a group interview with three participants from a fourth organization. Information about the respondents and their organizations are provided in Table 1. To avoid too much bias in our data by only interviewing people directly linked to the data science field, the group interview conducted by the second author was with people from an agile development team without data science experience. This gave us a more nuanced view of the data scientist role. Due to confidentiality agreements, further details about the organizations and their specific cases remain anonymous.

During the interviews, we presented our participants with our research topic and asked them to describe their experiences with data science, agile methods, team autonomy and experiences with implementing data scientist roles into agile teams. We followed the semi-structured approach, asking prepared questions but also allowing the conversations to naturally develop. During the former five interviews, detailed notes were taken, while the group interview was tape recorded based on consent and transcribed by the second author. After the interviews, the authors read through each other's notes and transcriptions, before discussing common topics that had emerged. Next, we separately coded the data. Due to the exploratory approach, the relatively short interview records, and low number of interviews we chose a holistic coding approach [16, 17]. As themes started to emerge, we discussed and resolved any disagreements in coding and interpretation.

Table 1. Data sources

Participants	Organization and team description
P1	Large private consultancy organization. Data scientist team lead, leading a team of two data scientists, 3–4 data engineers, one architect, one security architect
P2 and P3	Large public sector organization. P2 Lead for data scientist department. P3 data scientist
P4 and P5	Small start-up specialized in data scientist tasks. P4 CEO and data scientist team lead. P5 data scientist
Group interview	Three participants from a large public sector organization; one team leader, one tech lead and one interaction designer

3 Results

In this section, we present the results from the interviews, focusing on the main challenges with establishing the data scientist role in autonomous teams. Based on what our respondents told us, and discussion and analysis of the data between the two authors, six challenges and possible recommendations are summarized in Table 2.

Table 2. Main challenges identified during interviews

Challenges	Recommendation
1. Agile methods	Arrange team kick-off; allow time for the team to settle in and mature
2. The data scientist role	Provide training; Make a dictionary for key terms and expressions
3. Additional data roles	Adjust agile practices; What can be adapted to meet the needs of the DS? Adjust agile practices; What can be adapted to meet the needs of DS?
4. Creativity and freedom	Facilitate for Community of Practice (CoP)
5. Collaboration and knowledge sharing	Consider if additional "data roles" are needed
6. Data platforms and infrastructures	Build a data platform to gather data in one place

3.1 Agile Methods

Agile methods were employed to various degrees in all the respondents' teams. Although their perceptions varied, all of them also had some understanding of what it meant to be autonomous. Many used Scrum practices such as stand-up meetings, sprints and retrospectives. According to the data scientists in our sample, the usage of sprints could be challenging. P4 explained that it can be hard to work according to a sprint schedule, since a data scientist work out from hypotheses, which not always give something of value from a management and team lead point of view. However, as P4 stated, for a data scientist this provides insight about what is not working, and then can test other methods in the next sprint.

3.2   The Data Scientist Role

From the interviews it became quite clear that *"The definition of a data scientist has become more blurred"* (P1), and that this misconception lead to wrong expectations about what a team want the data scientist to solve, preventing the realization of the full value of having this role on the team. P3, also a data scientist, used her first months in the company working partially for different teams explaining what a data scientist is and what use-cases are suited for them to solve. In the group interview they claimed to have a data scientist on the team, but after we analyzed the interview it became clear that this role was actually a data analyst. They also explained that it could be hard to understand the terminology of the data scientist.

3.3   Additional Data Roles?

All respondents who held data scientist roles expressed that a data scientist in team should ideally be supported by a data engineer. P1, P4 and P5 explained that a data engineer's job is to create the infrastructure, so the data becomes easily available for the data scientist. Without data, it is hard for the data scientist to do their job. They further explained that teams lacking both roles might need to increase their total numbers of members with two or more. P3 said that one additional resource to the team might not be a big deal, but when first including one more resource, it is easy to add a couple more. However, according to P3, if there are too many resources on a team it can lose its autonomy.

3.4   Creativity and Freedom

To experiment and explore the data was highlighted as important for data scientists to thrive. For example, P3 explained that an important part of her job is to test and explore different hypotheses, and if the environment she works in is too rigid, it becomes difficult for her to do her job. This is also backed up by P1, P4 and P5. Although creativity and freedom are important, they also stated that management must point out the bigger problem they are going to solve. P4 explains that data scientists need a high degree of autonomy: *"A project manager should never tell a data scientist how to do things. Just tell them what are the overlaying problem that needs to be solved and when deadline is"*.

3.5   Collaboration and Knowledge Sharing

Collaboration and knowledge sharing among data scientist were also highlighted as important. P2, who leads a data scientist lab, stated that a data scientist should not allocate all its time to a team project, but also use time working together with other data scientists. This is important she said, because it is one of the best ways a data scientist can grow and learn. P3 explained that the time spent with other data scientist is valuable and is used to create and test different types of algorithms and make data science tools that can be reused across multiple projects. Along similar lines, the participants in the group interview expressed concern that their data analyst did not have sufficient opportunities for knowledge sharing with peers.

3.6   Data Platforms and Infrastructure

Data platforms and infrastructure was a final theme emerging from the interviews. All the data scientists expressed the need for easy access to data. Both P4 and P5 explained that a good infrastructure should be in place and that a data platform is necessary. Without it, it will be hard for the data scientist to do productive work and would use most of the time chasing data. This, they said, would not benefit neither the data scientist nor the team.

4   Discussion and Concluding Remarks

We now turn to discuss our research question *"What challenges do agile autonomous teams face in introducing data scientist roles into the team?"*.

We believe that understanding what a data scientist is and can do is key for a team to successfully incorporate the role. The confusion about the role, as seen from the group interview, can lead to sub-optimal use of the data scientist. This again can have negative effect both for the team and the data scientist. Therefore, it is important to train the team about what the data scientist can and should contribute with. It could be important that the team set a side time to manage expectations, both within the team and outwards to the rest of the organization. One way to manage expectations is to understand there may be different views of what value is. Often a team lead or manager have a different understanding of value than a data scientist. A machine learning implementation that after two weeks of work did not function as expected, would still in the data scientist eyes provide value in form of knowing what algorithms did not work so well and learn from the experience. However, a manager could see it as a failure and would struggle to find something of value. Therefore, when integrating new roles into the team, it might help the team to reflect upon the different aspects and views of value.

Also, an idea when building a data scientist environment might be to have data scientist partially in teams, and then train the teams in what use-cases is appropriate for a data scientist and help them understand the fields' terminology. Another suggestion is to arrange team kick-offs to work with specific data scientist use-cases, so the other team members becomes familiar with the topic. In a team kick-off one should also reflect on agile practices and if they need to be adapted to the inclusion of a data scientist.

One should also be mindful about other potential expansions of a team when including the data scientist role. A variety of roles could be needed, in addition to the data scientist, for a team to become data-driven [13]. An increased team size can lead to loss of team autonomy and agility [2]. Therefore, one should think carefully about if other roles must be added to support the new data scientist role. An alternative solution could be to see if current team members can be trained to take on additional roles.

Training current team members to become data scientist might not be feasible, as the role require high expertise of both statistics and programming skills. It would likely take a lot of time and investment to retrain a person for that role. For example, a data analyst might have the necessary statistical background but lack the programming experience, while a software developer lacks the mathematical background.

Alternatively, instead of focusing on training team members to become data scientists, it might be a better solution for the organization to train its members in skills which could help support the data scientist in its work. That way a team might avoid the increase in roles when adding a data scientist to the team. Instead of adding a couple of data engineers join the team, their tasks can be done by current team members, for example building a better infrastructure and provide the data scientist with an architectural overview.

Throughout the interviews, the importance of collaboration with other data scientists were highlighted. As pointed out by Davenport and Patil [12] there is a trade-off between working in cross-functional groups versus interaction with other specialists within their own field. Towards this end, organizations can establish Communities of Practice (CoP) where data scientists can exchange and discuss ideas, develop professional skills and new ways of working. CoP's are important for knowledge sharing, coordination and decision-making in large-scale agile development projects [18, 19]. An open data science CoP could contribute both to the data scientists' skill development, but also raising the understanding of other organizational members.

The creativity and freedom a data scientist require can be seen as the need for a high degree of individual autonomy. This notion is supported by Patil [15], but he does not say anything about how it might affect self-managing teams. In Moe et al. [7] the difficulty of balancing individual autonomy and team autonomy is discussed. They explain having greater redundancy in the team can reduce this problem. This redundancy the data scientist can use to engage in CoP's. Of course, one can also debate if the creativity and freedom the data scientists talk about in the interviews is the exact same kind of freedom and creativity any role in an autonomous team need. However, given the current popularity the data scientist role has in the industry it might be that it feels more natural for the data scientists to talk about it.

Although soft skills are necessary to succeed with implementing the data scientist role into the team, we cannot get by the fact that certain technical conditions must be fulfilled as well. A data-driven platform is a critical component in order to build an organization that aim to make data-driven decisions and utilize the competence of data scientists [20]. A platform is also seen as an important prerequisite for team autonomy [21]. Therefore, if traditional industries are going to succeed with integrating data scientist and let them work autonomous, it is important that they have access to all the data through a digital platform.

As a concluding remark, this is an ongoing study and the findings are preliminary. We recognize the important limitations, such as the use of a convenience sample and single-source design [17]. The fact that several of our respondents were data scientists themselves may represent a bias in the data gathered from the interviews. As mentioned in the method section, to nuance the sample we included the group interview with agile team members working with a data scientist. Further, the recommendations in Table 2 have not been validated and are only suggestions made by the authors. Future studies with more rigorous design and methods are needed in order to establish confidence in our findings. Future research could also include inter- and intra-team coordination, as team constellations including data scientist roles should be likely to be large-scale projects. Notwithstanding the limitations of this exploratory study, we believe more research-based knowledge on implementing data science roles in agile teams is important as organizations continue to make use of and combine data science and agile methods.

References

1. Larson, D., Chang, V.: A review and future direction of agile, business intelligence, analytics and data science. Int. J. Inf. Manag. **36**, 700–710 (2016)
2. Dikert, K., Paasivaara, M., Lassenius, C.: Challenges and success factors for large-scale agile transformations: a systematic literature review. J. Syst. Softw. **119**, 87–108 (2016). https://doi.org/10.1016/j.jss.2016.06.013
3. Kim, M., Zimmermann, T., DeLine, R., Begel, A.: The emerging role of data scientists on software development teams. Presented at the Proceedings of the 38th International Conference on Software Engineering (2016)
4. Stray, V., Moe, N.B., Hoda, R.: Autonomous agile teams: challenges and future directions for research. In: Proceedings of the 19th International Conference on Agile Software Development: Companion, p. 5. ACM, New York (2018)
5. Lee, G., Xia, W.: Toward agile: an integrated analysis of quantitative and qualitative field data on software development agility. MIS Q. **34**, 87–114 (2010)
6. Hoda, R., Noble, J., Marshall, S.: Self-organizing roles on agile software development teams. IEEE Trans. Softw. Eng. **39**, 422–444 (2013). https://doi.org/10.1109/TSE.2012.30
7. Moe, N.B., Dingsøyr, T., Dybå, T.: Overcoming barriers to self-management in software teams. IEEE Softw. **26**, 20–26 (2009)
8. Moe, N.B., Dingsøyr, T., Dybå, T.: A teamwork model for understanding an agile team: a case study of a Scrum project. Inf. Softw. Technol. **52**, 480–491 (2010)
9. Luger, G.F.: Artificial Intelligence: Structures and Strategies for Complex Problem Solving. Pearson education, London (2005)
10. Provost, F., Fawcett, T.: Data science and its relationship to big data and data-driven decision making. Big Data **1**, 51–59 (2013). https://doi.org/10.1089/big.2013.1508
11. Kunis: Data Analyst vs. Data Scientist (2018). https://www.springboard.com/blog/data-analyst-vs-data-scientist/
12. Davenport, T.H., Patil, D.: Data scientist. Harvard Bus. Rev. **90**, 70–76 (2012)
13. Fleming, O., Fountaine, T., Henke, N., Saleh, T.: Ten red flags signaling your analytics program will fail. https://www.mckinsey.com/business-functions/mckinsey-analytics/our-insights/ten-red-flags-signaling-your-analytics-program-will-fail
14. Davenport, T.H.: From analytics to artificial intelligence. J. Bus. Anal. 1–8 (2018). https://doi.org/10.1080/2573234X.2018.1543535
15. Patil, D.: Building Data Science Teams. O'Reilly Media, Newton (2011)
16. Saldaña, J.: The Coding Manual for Qualitative Researchers. Sage, Thousand Oaks (2012)
17. Yin, R.K.: Case Study Research and Applications: Design and Methods. Sage Publications, Thousand Oaks (2018)
18. Paasivaara, M., Lassenius, C.: Communities of practice in a large distributed agile software development organization – case Ericsson. Inf. Softw. Technol. **56**, 1556–1577 (2014). https://doi.org/10.1016/j.infsof.2014.06.008

19. Smite, D., Moe, N.B., Levinta, G., Floryan, M.: Spotify guilds: how to succeed with knowledge sharing in large-scale agile organizations. IEEE Softw. **36**, 51–57 (2019)
20. Segaran, T., Hammerbacher, J. (eds.): Beautiful Data: The Stories Behind Elegant Data Solutions. O'Reilly, Beijing, Sebastopol (2009)
21. Gundelsby, J.H.: Enabling autonomous teams in large-scale agile through architectural principles. In: Proceedings of the 19th International Conference on Agile Software Development: Companion, p. 17. ACM (2018)

Open Access This chapter is licensed under the terms of the Creative Commons Attribution 4.0 International License (http://creativecommons.org/licenses/by/4.0/), which permits use, sharing, adaptation, distribution and reproduction in any medium or format, as long as you give appropriate credit to the original author(s) and the source, provide a link to the Creative Commons license and indicate if changes were made.

The images or other third party material in this chapter are included in the chapter's Creative Commons license, unless indicated otherwise in a credit line to the material. If material is not included in the chapter's Creative Commons license and your intended use is not permitted by statutory regulation or exceeds the permitted use, you will need to obtain permission directly from the copyright holder.

The Influence of Culture and Structure on Autonomous Teams in Established Companies

Simone V. Spiegler[1,2(✉)], Christoph Heinecke[2], and Stefan Wagner[1]

[1] Institute of Software Technology, University of Stuttgart, Stuttgart, Germany
{simone.spiegler,stefan.wagner}@iste.uni-stuttgart.de
[2] Robert Bosch Automotive Steering GmbH, Schwäbisch Gmünd, Germany
Christoph.Heinecke@bosch.com

Abstract. *Motivation:* Many companies aim to provide more autonomy to their development teams. While some teams report on successes, others still struggle with the agile adaption, e.g. due to the organisational environment. *Objective:* Our objective was to explore how organisational culture and structure influence team autonomy in bureaucratic companies. *Method and Results:* 30 qualitative interviews from different business divisions at a conglomerate revealed that organisational factors related to hierarchy, specialist culture and functionally departmentalised structure decreased agile team features and consequently resulted in a reduced speed of decision-making. We suggest the Agile Matching Theory which implies that prevalent organisational factors and desired agile team features need to match to allow team autonomy to occur. *Conclusion:* We therefore encourage managers to further work on a learning organisation and a supportive structure within which autonomous teams can grow.

Keywords: Autonomous teams · Challenges · Bureaucracy

1 Introduction

Many companies started the agile transformation by implementing autonomous teams. Team autonomy implies to make team decisions regarding task allocation and execution as well as solve problems independently [12]. While narratives postulate great success stories on agile teams, empirical evidence often reveals how difficult it is for teams to work in an agile way [8,9,14].

Specifically teams in bureaucratic companies appear to face obstacles in working autonomously [1,17]. A mismatch between prevalent organisational factors and agile team behaviour was identified to serve as a major challenge for autonomous teams [9,15,21]. This paper specifically focuses on implementing autonomous teams in bureaucratic organisations. This type of organisation contradicts the agile way of working [17]. It is used to rely on a hierarchical culture

© The Author(s) 2019
R. Hoda (Ed.): XP 2019 Workshops, LNBIP 364, pp. 46–54, 2019.
https://doi.org/10.1007/978-3-030-30126-2_6

as opposed to autonomous teams [14], on rigid planning as opposed to iterative team learning [1] and on operating in a functional departmentalised structure as opposed to cross-functional teams [17]. Thus, we can assume that teams that aim at effectiveness struggle with working in an agile way if the necessary preconditions on the organisational level aim at supporting efficiency. Yet, scarce research examines the link between the organisational context and agile team behaviour [2,9,21]. Teams that are implemented in rather bureaucratic environments tend to struggle with working in an agile manner due to hindrances on the organisational level without the legitimate power to change their environment. To be able to support agile teams properly, management needs to know how organisational factors influence team behaviour. This study focuses on the influence of a bureaucratic environment on team autonomy. Our research question is therefore: *How do organisational culture and structure influence autonomy of teams?*

We have conducted semi-structured interviews with 30 individuals from 11 different Scrum teams at the Robert Bosch GmbH. Interviewees elaborated on successes but also on challenges. This study reports on the challenges with a specific focus on how the predominantly bureaucratic environment on the organisational level influences the agile way of working on the team level. Data revealed that a strong hierarchy, a specialist culture and functional departmentalised structures decreased agile team features such as psychological safety or team learning and consequently team autonomy. We suggest the Agile Matching Theory which implies a mandatory fit between prevalent organisational context and desired agile team features to enable teams to act autonomously.

2   Background

Agile teams are described to work cross-functionally within and across boundaries [3] with a high level of autonomy based on a common goal [2,22]. This paper considers the agile team features monitoring [16], psychological safety [5], team potency [18], shared mental models [13], team learning [5] and team orientation [16] to be predecessors of team autonomy.

Autonomy can be clustered into individual autonomy which provides a team member a high level of freedom regarding fulfilling a task [11], team autonomy which refers to shared decision making within teams and external autonomy related to interference by management [10]. External autonomy may not only refer to hierarchical culture [8,14,17], but also to a specialist culture [8,15] or to a functionally departmentalised structure including rigid processes [1,4,17] or geographical distribution [22].

Hoda and Noble [9] explain agile adaption by a link between organisational context and agile teams and call for further research on the dependency among the two levels of analysis. Yet, most research does not focus on exploring the relationship between organisational factors and its influence on team autonomy specifically. Furthermore, researchers tend to examine agile team challenges by mainly interviewing managerial positions [4,9].

We examined the influence of external autonomy on team autonomy by predominantly interviewing team members. Our results suggest the *Agile Matching Theory* which implies that team autonomy depends on the match between the prevalent external autonomy on the organisational level and desired agile team features. If the organisational context does not match with the required agile features on the team level, most likely team autonomy will be low (Table 1).

Table 1. Organisational factors and agile team factors

Bureaucratic organisation	Agile team factors
(1) Hierarchical culture [8,14,17]	Monitoring themselves [16]
	Psychological safety [5]
	Team potency [18]
(2) Specialist culture [8,15]	Shared mental models [13]
	Team learning [5]
	Team orientation [16]
(3) Functionally departmentalised [23]	Shared mental models [13]
	Team learning [5]
	Team orientation [16]
Reality: limited external autonomy	Desire: high team autonomy

Since contextual factors are mostly set by management [9,15] our results help managers to be aware of the boundary conditions teams should receive to be able to act autonomously.

3   Study Design

3.1   Research Context

We draw our sample from 5 different business divisions at the Robert Bosch GmbH. Founded in 1886 it became excellent in the bureaucratic way of working. Starting its agile journey in 2012 it is now in the middle of its transformation efforts. At present, some 410,000 employees are active in four different business areas each embracing multiple divisions with slightly different sub-cultures. While several divisions are already in the forefront of its agile transformation, others have started its journey just recently.

The sample contains 30 individuals from 11 different Scrum teams operating at 5 different business divisions, mainly active in the automotive industry. The sample contained 5 software and 6 non-software development project teams. We interviewed 6 Scrum Masters (SM), 4 Product Owners (PO) and 20 team members (TM). The age of projects ranged from 2 months up to 3 years. Team size ranged from 5 up to 12 members, often including individuals from different nationalities.

3.2   Data Collection and Analysis Procedure

We chose Grounded Theory because it allows for an exploratory approach in rather new scientific fields [7]. Additionally, we observed teams in their daily activities to understand the context of interviewees better. To answer the research question, we conducted qualitative semi-structured interviews of 45 min on average. We asked participants to elaborate on challenges concerning their current Scrum project. The questionnaire can be found online [19].[1] We audio-taped and transcribed each interview. We openly coded transcripts sentence-by-sentence and aligned codes that appeared to be alike to one concept and constantly reflected those concepts critically [7].

The organisational level contained the three categories high power distance, expert culture and functionally departmentalised structure which each consisted of a bundle of concepts. For example, the category *high power distance* involved the concepts *several hierarchical layers included in decision making, positional legitimacy* and *management overrules*. Those categories influenced six agile features on team level and decreased team autonomy.

Through constant comparison of various interviews we identified a mismatch between organisational factors and the core features of agile teams as major challenge in our research context. Based on three propositions we suggest *The Agile Matching Theory* which implies that a low team autonomy results from a misfit between prevalent organisational factors and desired agile team features.

Limitations: Since we only draw data from one company our results are limited to our research context and cannot be generalised. Thus, future testing of the propositions should draw data from different conglomerates. Furthermore, our findings are based on qualitative interviews and therefore, need to be confirmed by quantitative testing. More details on the recruitment of participants, the organisational context, validity procedure and limitations of the research are available elsewhere [20].

4   Findings

The findings describe challenges regarding organisational culture and structure and how each factor influenced autonomous teams.

Interviewees often mentioned that **organisational culture** linked to high power distance and specialised knowledge workers reduced external autonomy. **High power distance** was exemplified by several hierarchical layers which all needed to be included in decision-making processes even though some were said to not even add value, by management or Product Owner that felt to have the right to overrule team decisions or told the team what they had to do and by status legitimacy. As a result, sometimes team members reported to be frustrated, demotivated or to fear that management or Product Owner would overrule their

---

[1] The collected data are drawn from a broader research project on the Scrum Master role [20].

decisions anyways. Thus, low external autonomy resulted in a low level of self-monitoring, of psychological safety and of team potency. Which led to a lack of willingness and capability to make team decisions.

If think, maybe if the Product Owner would not tell me everyday what I have to do, maybe I would be more intrinsically motivated to do my tasks, maybe I would chose my tasks voluntarily. But like this. . . I just deliver a status report to my Product Owner every day! (TM)

But you don't necessarily receive decisions, you don't get information if you go there and say: hey, I am a team member of the agile team. If you go there as a common team member, you only get the information if you are in the proper hierarchical layer, only if you talk to a person at the same hierarchical level. That are the power plays. (TM)

We therefore suggest the following proposition:

> (P1) High power distance leads to a low level of team autonomy (1a). This relationship is moderated by monitoring (1b), psychological safety (1c) and team potency (1d).

A **specialist culture** was described by territories and by a lack in readiness to experiment. Some managers were said to prefer teams to follow a strict plan that was thoroughly thought through in advance and were reluctant to apply an inspect and adapt approach.

Territory refers to an expert who enjoys a sovereign right to keep specific knowledge and even the respective task all to him- or herself without sharing it. Therefore, other team members did not feel responsible or allowed to learn the specific knowledge. Interviewees also referred to a lack of willingness to learn things unrelated to the personal field of expertise or to a lack of discipline to not dig too deep into an expert topic.

Well, there are clearly defined areas in this team. Territories which are well hidden. You need some time to recognize them. [...] certain people are in certain territories which is simply inflexible. You realize this when there is one topic dropped, it is not considered. And than there are the people waiting and have nothing to do, even though there actually needs quite a lot to be done. Because there are the territories that you are not allowed to enter and than one does not work together. (SM)

While some team members appeared to own high individual autonomy regarding tasks, they had a low team autonomy. Thus, a specialist culture resulted in weak team learning, shared mental models and team orientation and consequently lead to low team autonomy. We therefore suggest the following proposition:

> (P2) A specialist culture leads to a low level of team autonomy (2a). This relationship is moderated by shared mental models (2b), team learning (2c) and team orientation (2d).

Some interviewees described the **organisational structure** as functionally departmentalised. It involved the categories departmental silos, department-oriented goals, geographical distribution and rigid processes.

Teams reported that they had to rely on external know-how due to processes which slowed them down. Some teams that depended on external support had difficulties in receiving a timely response or even at all.

If a team is not both at the same time - a self-organized team and the company itself - you always need interfaces, stuff from other people. And especially big companies are often divided into silos, which makes it very very difficult. You always need to wait for stuff. You ask for something and then you don't get it. And you do something, you show it to someone and then they don't respond. [...] or because they simply don't have time to respond. (PO)

Sometimes, different sprint goals or contrasting departmental goals resulted in slow decision-making. For example, purchasing would try to reduce costs while developers searched for the technically best solution which would be more expensive. Some agile teams reported to clash with traditional teams that followed a classic project plan in contrast to iterative learning. Those neighbouring project teams were considered to be slow and inflexible in relation to agile teams, which made it difficult to synchronise project goals and milestones. Interviewees also said that it was a challenge to include external experts for the up-coming sprint in advance. Furthermore, geographical distribution limited knowledge exchange, synchronisation of progress, visualisation, discussions about critical topics and decision making.

Therefore, a functionally departmentalised structure resulted in weak shared understanding, team learning and team orientation. This leads to slow team decision-making. We suggest the following proposition:

> (P3) A functional departmentalised structure leads to a low level of team autonomy (3a). This relationship is moderated by shared mental models (3b), team learning (3c) and team orientation (3d).

5 Implication for Research and Practice

We found that high power distance, specialist culture and a functional departmentalised structure decreased team autonomy. Since people behave according to the context within which they operate [2] we suggest that teams can only act autonomously if they face the necessary preconditions on the organisational level. For example, management can destroy the self-organising nature easily (e.g. [8, 9, 14]) by making decisions on behalf of the team. Therefore, even though companies aim at implementing agile teams, team autonomy will remain low when a company does not simultaneously provide a high level of external autonomy by changing the organisational culture and structure.

The agile way of working is based on shared values, believes and a common goal, a normative approach while bureaucratic organisations are based on written rules, standards, processes. Therefore, established companies that have already started its agile transformation by implementing agile teams have to increase its efforts even further to empower real autonomous teams by putting even more effort into changing the organisational structure and culture.

We have observed several promising initiatives in established companies to start an agile transformation by setting up autonomous teams in protected yet even isolated clusters. Providing a guarded environment to let teams, management and the surrounding structures try, experiment, learn and accept new ways of collaboration for too long brings the risk that those "islands" will only exist as such. Established companies that have made first experience with working in an agile way and that have created valuable insights must take the next challenging step to introduce their individual learning episodes to a broader organisational level and to expand their activities to those structures that seemed not ready yet, by providing similar values, believes as well as goal setting and to nourish from the success of their protected test teams.

Companies should foster a learning organisation [6] that encourages employees to continuously share knowledge openly and to learn from each other unrelated to their position or functional structure. This requires tools and communities to allow for transparency, e.g. social business platforms that are easily accessible. The opportunity to contribute and to be acknowledged for knowledge sharing among team members and communities intrinsically motivates individuals and fosters team learning and creativity [22]. Therefore, management needs to foster knowledge management tools and experiments to incentive those that actively share or promote knowledge and to provide more work time for communities of practice and open space meetings.

The Scrum method suggests dedicated full-time team members that own all competences needed to fulfil a given task. Yet, since this is often not possible: In reality teams have to call in experts according to their sprint goals. This requires an open organisation with easy access to different competences and skills.

We contribute to existing research by providing more insights on how organisational factors can challenge team autonomy. While many companies report on success stories on autonomous teams this research provides a brief insight on the challenges. This study is one further step to help management understand how culture and structure limit autonomy of agile teams. More research is needed to understand supporting and hindering factors and to how they apply in reality.

References

1. Boehm, B., Turner, R.: Management challenges to implementing agile processes in traditional development organizations. IEEE Softw. **22**(5), 30–39 (2005)
2. Cockburn, A., Highsmith, J.: Agile software development, the people factor. Computer **34**(11), 131–133 (2001)
3. Conboy, K.: Agility from first principles: reconstructing the concept of agility in information systems development. Inf. Syst. Res. **20**(3), 329–354 (2009)
4. Conboy, K., Coyle, S., Wang, X., Pikkarainen, M.: People over process: key people challenges in agile development. IEEE Softw. **28**(4), 47–57 (2011)
5. Edmondson, A.: Psychological safety and learning behavior in work teams. Adm. Sci. Q. **44**(2), 350–383 (1999)
6. Garvin, D.A., Edmondson, A.C., Gino, F.: Is yours a learning organization? Harvard Bus. Rev. **86**(3), 109 (2008)
7. Glaser, B.G., Strauss, A.L.: Discovery of Grounded Theory: Strategies for Qualitative Research. Routledge, Abingdon (2017)
8. Hoda, R., Murugesan, L.K.: Multi-level agile project management challenges: a self-organizing team perspective. J. Syst. Softw. **117**, 245–257 (2016)
9. Hoda, R., Noble, J.: Becoming agile: a grounded theory of agile transitions in practice. In: Proceedings of the 39th International Conference on Software Engineering, ICSE 2017, Piscataway, NJ, USA, pp. 141–151. IEEE Press (2017). https://doi.org/10.1109/ICSE.2017.21
10. Hoegl, M., Parboteeah, P.: Autonomy and teamwork in innovative projects. Hum. Resour. Manag. **45**(1), 67–79 (2006)
11. Langfred, C.W.: The paradox of self-management: individual and group autonomy in work groups. J. Organ. Behav. **21**(5), 563–585 (2000)
12. Leach, D.J., Wall, T.D., Rogelberg, S.G., Jackson, P.R.: Team autonomy, performance, and member job strain: uncovering the teamwork KSA link. Appl. Psychol. **54**(1), 1–24 (2005)
13. Levesque, L.L., Wilson, J.M., Wholey, D.R.: Cognitive divergence and shared mental models in software development project teams. J. Organ. Behav. **22**(2), 135–144 (2001)
14. Moe, N.B., Aurum, A., Dybå, T.: Challenges of shared decision-making: a multiple case study of agile software development. Inf. Softw. Technol. **54**(8), 853–865 (2012)
15. Moe, N.B., Dingsøyr, T., Dybå, T.: Overcoming barriers to self-management in software teams. IEEE Softw. **26**(6), 20–26 (2009)
16. Moe, N.B., Dingsøyr, T., Dybå, T.: A teamwork model for understanding an agile team: a case study of a scrum project. Inf. Softw. Technol. **52**(5), 480–491 (2010)
17. Nerur, S., Mahapatra, R.K., Mangalaraj, G.: Challenges of migrating to agile methodologies. Commun. ACM **48**(5), 72–78 (2005)
18. Schmidt, C.: Agile Software Development Teams. Springer, Heidelberg (2016). https://doi.org/10.1007/978-3-319-26057-0
19. Spiegler, S.V., Heinecke, C., Wagner, S.: Interview Guidelines for "Leadership Gap in Agile Teams: How Teams and Scrum Masters Mature" (2018). https://doi.org/10.5281/zenodo.2243113
20. Spiegler, S.V., Heinecke, C., Wagner, S.: Leadership gap in agile teams: how teams and scrum masters mature. In: Kruchten, P., Fraser, S., Coallier, F. (eds.) XP 2019. LNBIP, vol. 355, pp. 37–52. Springer, Cham (2019). https://doi.org/10.1007/978-3-030-19034-7_3

21. Stray, V., Moe, N.B., Hoda, R.: Autonomous agile teams: challenges and future directions for research. In: Proceedings of the 19th International Conference on Agile Software Development: Companion, XP 2018, pp. 16:1–16:5. ACM, New York (2018). https://doi.org/10.1145/3234152.3234182
22. Takeuchi, H., Nonaka, I.: The new new product development game. Harvard Bus. Rev. **64**(1), 137–146 (1986)
23. Weber, M.: The Theory of Social and Economic Organization. Simon and Schuster, New York (2009)

Open Access This chapter is licensed under the terms of the Creative Commons Attribution 4.0 International License (http://creativecommons.org/licenses/by/4.0/), which permits use, sharing, adaptation, distribution and reproduction in any medium or format, as long as you give appropriate credit to the original author(s) and the source, provide a link to the Creative Commons license and indicate if changes were made.

The images or other third party material in this chapter are included in the chapter's Creative Commons license, unless indicated otherwise in a credit line to the material. If material is not included in the chapter's Creative Commons license and your intended use is not permitted by statutory regulation or exceeds the permitted use, you will need to obtain permission directly from the copyright holder.

Agile Autonomous Teams in Complex Organizations

Marius Mikalsen[1,2]([✉]), Magne Næsje[2], Erik André Reime[2], and Anniken Solem[1,2]

[1] SINTEF Digital, Trondheim, Norway
marius.mikalsen@sintef.no
[2] Norwegian University of Science and Technology, Trondheim, Norway

Abstract. In complex organizations, the effective functioning of autonomous teams is challenged by the need to coordinate and align work with multiple experts and other units in the organization. We report on the challenges experienced in an agile program consisting of cross-functional teams set up with resources from both the IT and business development side of the organization, while team members simultaneously remain in their line organization. Through an empirical case study of the agile program, we find that the production structure (i.e. the distribution of operational tasks) and the control structure (i.e. managing activities related to the operational task) influence agile team autonomy. We contribute by pushing past describing dependencies in terms of coordination challenges and mechanisms. To do this, we use modern sociotechnical theory to discuss how a production structure with many dependencies cause challenges and how a misaligned control structure is time-consuming and reduces team autonomy.

Keywords: Agile · Autonomous teams · Complex organizations · Case study · Modern sociotechnical theory

1 Introduction

With increased digitalization, organizations face rapid changes in customer demands, changing markets, and continuous technological advancements. It forces established, traditional non-agile, complex organizations to make their software development more agile. By complex, we depict an organization with many units, with dependencies amongst them. The number of units and the strength of the dependencies determines the complexity. Traditionally, bureaucracy, plans, and hierarchies have addressed complexity. Agile ways of working are different, and extant research has not sufficiently addressed the issue of introducing agile autonomous teams within complex organizations [1, 2]. Introducing agile teams in a complex organization will cause challenging dependencies on condition that the surrounding organization remains plan based and hierarchical [3]. However, our knowledge of how such dependencies influence the autonomy of agile teams is limited, hence our RQ: *How is complexity in organizations influencing the autonomy of agile teams?*

© The Author(s) 2019
R. Hoda (Ed.): XP 2019 Workshops, LNBIP 364, pp. 55–63, 2019.
https://doi.org/10.1007/978-3-030-30126-2_7

We answer this question through an empirical case study of an agile program (henceforth referred to as AP) consisting of autonomous agile teams within a bank. The teams in AP are cross-functional, being staffed with personnel from both business and IT units. The number of dependencies between people, tasks, knowledge, technical assets, and other resources makes this a complex organization.

To analyze our findings, we use modern sociotechnical theory (henceforth referred to as MST). MST is concerned with meeting dynamic business environments by designing flexible organizations. MST problematizes structural issues of production and control, and in this case, how these influence agile autonomous teams.

2 Theoretical Background

Agile and Autonomous Teams

Team autonomy and diversity is reported to be key in achieving agility [4]. The process of forming and implementing teams with high autonomy, as well as the effective functioning of such teams, are not yet adequately addressed and understood in the context of complex organizations [5]. To understand autonomous teams in complex environments, it is crucial to understand the organizational context surrounding the team as it is an important determinant of effectiveness [6], effecting the potential for autonomy. Thus, there is a need for new knowledge on how to organize for and utilize autonomous teams, in order to attain better performance, productivity, innovation and value creation, hence increase competitiveness.

Agile autonomous Teams in Complex Organizations

While agile and autonomous teams have shown success in smaller projects, introducing such teams in complex organizations is known to be challenging [1]. Complex organizations are more challenging because there are many dependencies, which traditionally have been controlled through plans, hierarchies and standardization [2]. Dependencies exist between agile teams, and from agile teams to the rest of the organization [7]. As agile and autonomous teams are introduced within complex organizations, it may be problematic to scale agile coordination and communication practices from the team level, as such a change requires a change in organizational structure and processes [8].

When introducing agile teams in an organization that is otherwise traditionally organized, this can imply that the teams are being restricted by the rest of the organization operating in plan and waterfall mode [8]. This has led some suggest that it is necessary that all departments "transform" if one is to gain full benefit from agile [3]. It seems that new insight on how to deal with complex interactions and dependencies is required [7, 9], as discussed next.

Modern Sociotechnical Theory (MST) as a Lens on Dependencies

The motivation behind modern sociotechnical theory (MST) is meeting dynamic business environments (e.g. rapidly changing user behaviors and technology) by designing flexible organizations. A flexible organization is achieved by creating complex jobs within simple organizations [10]. This approach is similar to the thinking behind agile ways of working and autonomous teams. Bureaucratic organizations, due to their focus on maximum division of labor and central control over core work processes, do not fare well in dynamic environments [11].

Originating from a tradition focusing on how organizations are structured, MST puts emphasis on how structural complexity (e.g., the degree of team dependency towards other teams and functional units) in organizations influences team autonomy and production [12]. The theory describes how disturbances (i.e. unplanned events) originate from dependencies that can be traced to the configuration of the organizational structure.

MST divides the organizational structure into production and control structure [10]. The production structure describes the distribution of operational tasks across actors, and their relation (e.g. a business developer and a software developer cooperating to develop a new feature). The control structure describes the distribution of regulatory tasks, that is, managing activities related to the operational task (e.g. a PO managing the above-mentioned development). A job entails a set of operational and regulatory tasks.

When the handling of disturbances to production involves actors outside the task (such as a manager), it is considered an external regulation. When the handling is within the task without interfering with the environment, it is considered an internal regulation. At the core of MST is a two-step structural redesign [11]. The first step is to create a production structure with few dependencies that minimize disturbances. Second, the goal of the control structure is to decentralize decision making-authority, creating an amplified regulatory potential (i.e. ability to perform regulatory tasks) that is aligned with operational tasks (e.g. enabling teams' opportunity to handle remaining disturbances). MST has concepts for understanding organizational structures, dependencies, and disturbances. Thus, it can be used to deepen our understanding of agile autonomous teams established in complex organizations.

3   Case and Method

Case Background
This study is a part of a longitudinal interpretative case study [13] of agile autonomous teams set in a Norwegian bank (dubbed NorBank for anonymity), with more than 2,000 employees. NorBank initiated in 2017 an agile program (AP) consisting of five cross-functional autonomous teams organized in line with agile principles, with the goal of developing improved software for their business-to-business solutions in the insurance market. The teams consist of resources from both the IT and business development side of the organization. A product owner (PO), who is responsible for realizing the team's delivery and goals, as well as managing the customer relationship, leads each team. Importantly, and which is often the case in complex organizations, members of the teams remained organized in a line organization (such as the IT and business side) and partake in several projects simultaneously. Therefore, the teams are staffed with part-time resources, particularly from the IT side. AP is managed by a group consisting of relevant IT and business managers from NorBank units which AP interfaces with. The

POs and a business architect also participate in this management group. NorBank has a set of legacy systems to which the solutions developed by the AP depends.

Data Collection and Analysis
The empirical data was collected in four rounds, using semi-structured interviews, observations of retrospectives carried out in AP and feedback sessions (Table 1). In order to qualitatively analyze our empirical findings, we used the stepwise deductive-inductive method (SDI) [14]. The inductive purpose of the SDI-method is to move from raw data, through categories, to concepts or theories. This is done by first encoding (i.e. writing words or phrases that describe paragraphs or even smaller sections of the data material) the data in a manner that retains the details of the original material. The next step is to systematize the codes that are relevant to the research question into categories. Finally, concepts are developed by applying relevant theory to the categories.

To increase the validity of our research, two of the researchers that created the codes first carried out the data coding individually. The data from the first round of the data collection resulted in 383 codes, and the second round gave 231 codes. The "NVivo 12 Pro"-software was used in the coding process. After the coding, the researchers created inductive categories based on the codes. This resulted in 21 categories for the first round and 12 categories for the second. By applying the MST lens, the findings were organized into two main categories, production structure and control structure. Combined, these categories provide insight on the dependencies occurring with agile teams in complex organizations. The purpose of the two last rounds of data collection was to saturate the categories. Feedback sessions were used to present the intermediary results to the case.

Table 1. Collected data

Data sources	Participants
25 interviews	Head of AP, IT managers, business managers, business architect, POs, IT developers, IT analysts and business developers
4 observations	Management group meeting and retrospective (2), PO meeting and retrospective, and a team retrospective
2 feedback sessions	Head of AP and business manager, AP's management group

4   Findings

Production Structure: AP has dependencies to its surrounding non-agile organization, thus resulting in a complex production structure. The dependencies are in relation to the IT and business units in NorBank, as well as personnel working on core and business systems on which AP systems rely.

AP's dependency towards the IT-side of the organization proved particularly challenging, as AP uses shared IT-resources. While IT-resources work in AP, they also have tasks in other projects and in their own units. When one PO is asked about the effects of having shared resources, the answer is: *"Having resources that aren't 100% (dedicated) is clearly a challenge. [...] If they have line tasks, then their mind is on that and not the project (AP), it is something we have to work with."* A team member in AP also reflects this diverging focus: *"I work 50%, 50%, 40% (distributed between AP, department and another project). [...] It's chaotic working with so much at the same time. [...] You don't feel like you get to do your job satisfactorily."* AP's dependency towards the IT-departments through shared resources gives rise to structurally conditioned disturbances. A PO illustrates this disturbance: *"Often there is something that, 'we just have to fix tomorrow' or customer issue or that kind of thing that is prioritized over everything else. The consequence is that you get fewer resources in the flows (AP teams)."*

AP develops software solutions meant for business-to-business units of NorBank, such as sales and customer service. The business side knows the customer, and is sometimes the customer of the solutions developed by AP. AP needs to mobilize resources from the business side to understand the software's functional requirements. A PO describes this process: *"When we start developing a new module, we assess who is to be included in a workgroup (from the business side), lead by one of our (the teams') business developers. We have to fetch those who are on the phone with customers."* A manager from the business side indicates that such work is not always prioritized: *"Many (POs) wish that more (from the business side) were hands-on and involved. [...] But we are not there that it is prioritized."*

There are also dependencies to personnel with knowledge and responsibility for the core and business systems. These systems constitute the underlying IT-infrastructure, on which business systems are built. A PO indicates how this can be time-consuming: *"This takes time. [...] We, together with [a core team], develop [a new system], but you also have those who work with the business systems. [...] They have completely different prioritizations."*

In sum, AP's production structure has many dependencies to the surrounding organization, which as shown have diverging prioritizations. This creates disturbances that influence the AP-teams' ability to be autonomous and agile. Thus, the production structure gives rise to challenges regarding who controls the resources.

Control Structure: AP's control structure functions so that AP teams, through their respective POs, have a regulatory potential that is internally high, and externally low, as illustrated below.

The POs have a high regulatory potential internally through trust from the management group. Due to the dedication of internal decision-making authority to POs, the AP-teams have adapted their work methods and a coordination layer within the AP has been removed. An IT-manager describes trust as an important factor: *"I think it's an important factor for the teams and those leading the teams that we [the management group] give them trust, in regards to us being confident that they work with the right stuff."* One of the POs also expresses this trust: *"I feel that we are very autonomous in the team. If we want to do it this way or that way, it's just up to us to decide it."*

Externally, on the other hand, the POs are responsible for handling several dependencies. When asked about the POs negotiation power and understanding of the surrounding organization, a manager from the business side answers: *"It is a very important factor. [...] You are supposed to deliver something to many (stakeholders).*

Or, a lot of people that care. The maneuvering of the stakeholder map, in that way, is demanding." The low external regulatory potential is indicated by the fact that the POs themselves do not have control over the resource allocation from the IT side, the priorities of the business side, and resources in core and business systems. A PO illustrates the lack of control over resource allocation from the IT side: *"The only thing I can't do anything about is the team members and how many percent they are allocated to the team. That is, in a way, beyond my control."* Another PO describes how this takes time: *"The project took a lot of time last year before we had any progress because we were staffed wrong."* An extra dimension to the team challenge with shared resources, is that the employees are highly autonomous in their work prioritization, as one IT-analyst confirms when asked about who decides where work should be done: *"There is nothing given at all. [...] I decide myself."* The above illustrates how POs need to handle both IT-managers and –resources in AP's dependency to IT units.

A PO describes how the dependency towards the business side and their prioritization cause disturbances hindering the AP-teams' effectiveness: *"If you meet a service-minded person, like we did when needing [type of insurance], it is done 'in seconds'. And if you meet someone different, like we did [another type of insurance], it takes like a month."*

The dependency on core and business systems personnel is also a hindrance, according to one PO: *"What also limits our effectiveness is unstable test systems. [...] the test systems were down for 1,5 week. [...] I felt that no one listened when I brought it up."*

In sum, the above indicates how the control structure does not give enough external regulatory potential to enable handling of disturbances. Thus, the control structure does not align with the complex production structure.

5   Discussion

Extant research shows that there are challenges related to dependencies between agile autonomous teams and a surrounding complex organization [1, 7]. However, empirical insight on the particularities of these challenges is scarce. Driven by our research question - how is complexity in organizations influencing the autonomy of agile teams – we have reported findings from an empirical case study of a bank that has established an agile program consisting of autonomous cross-functional teams within a complex organizational setting. Our findings indicate how production structure and control structure influence the autonomy of teams. We find how the AP has a high degree of internal regulatory potential (i.e. shaping the inner life of the program), while the external regulatory potential is lower (e.g. regulating access to resources). These findings contribute to the existing literature on agile autonomous teams in complex organizations as we discuss.

First, in terms of production structure, we find that not all production resources are embedded in the AP, which leads to a reliance on shared resources. This creates external dependencies, which we find are time-consuming to handle and hence reduce the autonomy of teams. This adds to the findings from [7], as a form of negotiation that takes place between autonomous teams and the surrounding organization. While having full-time resources dedicated to teams is common in many organizations, we expect that having shared production resources with many dependencies is more common in complex organizations adopting agile methods. MST [10] suggests reducing such dependencies by organizational redesign moving more resources that are full-time into the autonomous teams. Such redesign of organizational structures is also what Dikert et al. [3] suggest. Changing the surrounding organizational structure to fit agile, is somewhat different from Barlow et al. [2], who suggest tailoring methods depending on the size of the project and the nature of the dependencies. We cannot conclude on what is the best course of action, if there exists one, but illustrate how there are different ways of approaching the challenges of dependencies.

Second, we find that AP has a high level of internal regulatory potential by having sufficient levels of control of the inner workings of the agile program, such as how work is organized, what tasks that are prioritized etc. However, the dependence on resources that are outside of AP, such as shared IT resources, lowers the external regulatory potential. Low external regulatory potential, our findings show, is time-consuming and limits the autonomy of the teams in AP. This is in line with other research on how plan based and waterfall managed surroundings is a restricting factor upon interfacing agile teams [8]. Some suggest that it is necessary that all departments transform towards agile if one is to gain the full benefits [3]. An additional insight from MST [10] is that the degree to which external dependencies influence autonomous teams' production capacity is dependent on the level of control the teams have in terms of regulating disturbances. With shared resources, control, i.e. the ability to regulate potential disturbances, may well be, at least partially, outside the agile autonomous teams' control, and potentially influence production capacity.

Finally, there are also some practical implications we can draw from our analysis. First, according to MST [10], creating such agile programs should start by creating a production structure with as few dependencies as possible. One way to do this is to, as far as possible without negative consequences to the rest of the organization, staff the agile programs with full-time resources. Second, if the organization cannot provide full-time resources into agile programs, it would be beneficial if the units having resources in the program also use agile ways of working. Then the shift from working in the agile program and the units will be less time-consuming. Third, resources working on core systems often become bottlenecks and create time-consuming dependencies. One way to remedy this would be to aim to give a sufficient level of resources experience and training in such systems. This involves giving developers enough time to develop in-depth knowledge of core systems.

6 Conclusion and Recommendations for Future Work

In this paper, we have analyzed the establishment of agile autonomous teams in a complex organization. A perspective on the alignment of production and control structure relating to dependencies and disturbances can provide new insights on agile team autonomy in complex organizations. First, it would be interesting to investigate the alignment of production and control structures in organizations that have done full-scale agile transformations, that is, moved towards fully autonomous teams. Such studies could be used for comparison towards cases where only parts are transformed, as reported in this case. Second, we have only begun to describe the role of production and control structures relating to agile autonomous teams in complex organizations, so there is a need for more in-depth studies to flesh out this phenomenon. Third, in our analysis, part-time resources is a prime source of disturbances. However, it will be necessary to investigate other sources of disturbances, such as technical dependencies, and see how they can be controlled. Finally, it seems relevant to investigate the level of control necessary for teams in order to regulate disturbances and be able to act autonomously.

References

1. Kruchten, P.: Contextualizing agile software development. J. Softw. Evol. Process **25**(4), 351–361 (2013)
2. Barlow, J.B., et al.: Overview and guidance on agile development in large organizations. Commun. Assoc. Inf. Syst. **29**, 25–44 (2011)
3. Dikert, K., Paasivaara, M., Lassenius, C.: Challenges and success factors for large-scale agile transformations: a systematic literature review. J. Syst. Softw. **119**, 87–108 (2016)
4. Lee, G., Xia, W.: Toward agile: an integrated analysis of quantitative and qualitative field data on software development agility. MIS Q. **34**(1), 87–114 (2010)
5. Mathieu, J., Maynard, M.T., Rapp, T., Gilson, L.: Team effectiveness 1997–2007: a review of recent advancements and a glimpse into the future. J. Manag. **34**(3), 410–476 (2008)
6. Hackman, J.R.: The design of work teams. In: Lorch, J. (ed.) Handbook of Organizational Behavior, pp. 315–342. Prentice Hall, Englewood Cliffs (1987)
7. Mikalsen, M., Moe, N.B., Stray, V., Nyrud, H.: Agile digital transformation: a case study of interdependencies. In: Thirty Ninth International Conference on Information Systems, San Francisco (2018)
8. Khan, M.R., Fernandez, W.D., Jiang, J.J.: Is there such a thing as agile IT program management? In: International Research Workshop on IT Project Management (2016)
9. Rolland, K.H., Fitzgerald, B., Dingsøyr, T., Stol, K.-J.: Problematizing agile in the large: alternative assumptions for large-scale agile development. In: 37th International Conference on Information systems (ICIS), Dublin (2016)
10. de Sitter, U., Den Hertog, J.F., Dankbaarl, B.: From complex organizations with simple jobs to simple organizations with complex jobs. Hum. Relat. **50**(5), 497–534 (1997)
11. van Amelsvoort, P., van Hootegem, G.: Towards a total workplace innovation concept based on sociotechnical systems design. In: Oeij, P., Rus, D., Pot, F.D. (eds.) Workplace Innovation. AHSW, pp. 281–299. Springer, Cham (2017). https://doi.org/10.1007/978-3-319-56333-6_17

12. Vriens, D., Achterbergh, J.: Cybernetically sound organizational structures I: de Sitter's design theory. Kybernetes **40**(3/4), 405–424 (2011)
13. Klein, H.K., Myers, M.D.: A set of principles for conducting and evaluating interpretative field studies in information systems. MIS Q. **23**(1), 67–88 (1999)
14. Tjora, A.H.: Kvalitative forskningsmetoder i praksis. Gyldendal akademisk, Oslo (2012)

Open Access This chapter is licensed under the terms of the Creative Commons Attribution 4.0 International License (http://creativecommons.org/licenses/by/4.0/), which permits use, sharing, adaptation, distribution and reproduction in any medium or format, as long as you give appropriate credit to the original author(s) and the source, provide a link to the Creative Commons license and indicate if changes were made.

The images or other third party material in this chapter are included in the chapter's Creative Commons license, unless indicated otherwise in a credit line to the material. If material is not included in the chapter's Creative Commons license and your intended use is not permitted by statutory regulation or exceeds the permitted use, you will need to obtain permission directly from the copyright holder.

Earn Your Wings: A Novel Approach to Deployment Governance

Yvan Petit[1(✉)] and Carl Marnewick[2]

[1] Business School of University of Quebec at Montreal, Montreal, Canada
`petit.yvan@uqam.ca`
[2] University of Johannesburg, Johannesburg, South Africa

Abstract. This paper presents a model to assess team autonomy developed and deployed in a South African bank's IT department. The bank has been deploying SAFe® for the last two years and in the process has increased significantly the number of software releases. Historically, the teams had to obtain multiple levels of authorization prior to a release but this level of governance and control was contradictory to the principle of team empowerment at the core of agile approaches. The model is inspired from the theme of a pilot's ability to fly an aircraft using five levels. The level is determined based on team fly-ability and elevation safety described in detail in this paper. Team fly-ability includes two elements: (1) maturity of engineering practices and (2) the ability to manage traceability and risk through ease of recovery. Elevation Safety is based on two components: (1) historical data on deployment performance and severity of incidents and (2) the application dynamics and criticality. The main benefits of this program are improved accountability of teams, reduced approval time, and reduced attempts to find workarounds and loopholes.

Keywords: Scaling agile · Team autonomy · Deployment · Governance

1 Introduction

More and more large organizations are now adopting agile enterprise-wide. However, the scaling of agile to a larger undertaking, creates an entire new set of problems and challenges ranging from resistance to change to the problems associated with hierarchical management and organizational boundaries. Leffingwell [1] groups the challenges of scaling agile into two broad categories: (1) those inherent to the methods themselves, "because of the fixed rule bases and assumptions built into the methods" (p. 87); and (2) challenges imposed by the enterprise that "will prevent the successful application of the new methods" (p. 87). More recently, Dikert, Paasivaara and Lassenius [2] surveyed 52 publications describing 42 industrial cases and reported 35 challenges grouped in nine categories: change resistance, lack of investment, agile difficult to implement, coordination challenged in multi-team environment, different approaches emerge in a multi-team environment, hierarchical management and organizational boundaries, requirement engineering challenges, quality assurance challenges, integrating non-development functions. Surprisingly, very little empirical research has been done on how to alleviate these challenges [3].

© The Author(s) 2019
R. Hoda (Ed.): XP 2019 Workshops, LNBIP 364, pp. 64–71, 2019.
https://doi.org/10.1007/978-3-030-30126-2_8

However, consultancy firms have developed various frameworks and models to address these challenges to implement scaled agile: Disciplined Agile Framework [4], Large Scale Scrum (LeSS) [5] and Nexus [6]. The most popular framework for scaling agile remains SAFe [6–8].

All these frameworks are building on the values and principles of the agile manifesto [9], among others the deployment and support of self-organized teams. Although much has been researched on teams, particularly in the field of psychology, much remains to be investigated in the context of agile deployment. The objective of this paper is therefore to contribute to the field, based on a research question proposed, during last year's workshop on scaling agile at XP 2018 [10]: *What is the right degree of team autonomy in different contexts (and how to measure it)?*"

2 Literature Review

Parker, Holesgrove, and Pathak [11] define a self-organized team "as a self-regulated, semi-autonomous small group of employees whose members determine, plan and manage their day-to-day activities and duties under reduced or no supervision." (p. 112) and the labels "autonomous teams" have been used as synonyms for "self-organizing teams," "self-managing teams" and "empowered teams" [10].

Teams have been studied for decades, primarily in the field of psychology. Literature abounds on numerous topics such as: leadership, roles, phases, performance, team dynamics, etc. More and more researchers reuse some of that literature to study software development teams using agile approaches, for example to relate autonomy to team performance [12], empowerment and outcomes in software development organizations [13], productivity of self-organized teams [11] and job satisfaction and/or motivation [14].

However, according to Kakar [15] "no approach or instrument has yet been designed to measure and compare self-organization between teams. Second, although conceptually the difference in adoption of self-organization in agile versus plan-driven methods has been discussed previously in the literature, the levels of self-organization between these two major paradigms of software development have not been objectively compared" (p. 208). In the case presented in this paper, the issue was the assessment of the teams and the level of authority delegated to them by the senior management. This is what Cao, Mohan, Xu and Ramesh classified as "sources of structure" in their proposed framework.

3 Methodology

The development and deployment of a new model to assess teams in order to grant them the right level of autonomy to release software was observed in a large South African bank's IT department. Twenty employees in the department were interviewed. The interviews were conducted by the two researchers themselves. The twenty interviewees comprised of four people from business who were direct customers of IT and ultimately the agile process, two people from the agile portfolio office, four portfolio project managers, the CFO of the IT department, two CIOs within the IT department, three release train engineers, one COO and three agile coaches.

Most of the interviews were directed towards understanding the link between the IT initiatives and the organization's strategy. However, during the course of the research many interviewees kept referring to an internal program to assess a team's autonomy with respect to the deployment of software. There were two interviews with the people responsible for the deployment and improvement of engineering practices. The interviews were coded in ATLAS.ti to assist in the analysis and summary of the approach. The objective of this paper is primarily to present and share an experience report from the perspective of the bank with the understanding that their approach might be of interest to other organizations.

4   Case Description

SA Bank (Note: This is a fictitious name to protect the identity of the bank), a financial institution, is one of the largest African financial institutions by assets. SA Bank is among the largest organizations in South Africa by market capitalization. It offers a wide range of banking and financial services to millions of personal customers in 20 African countries. The company employs over 6000 people in their IT.

SA Bank decided to start deploying agile practices in their IT department. They redesigned their software development completely and restructured around self-organizing teams responsible for products rather than specific activities. These teams would also be in close contact with business representatives and would be entirely responsible for the development, testing, deployment, and maintenance of their products. The intention was to reduce the number of handoffs and simplify the development process dramatically. The SAFe deployment was strongly committed to and supported by executives and line managers across the board.

At the time of the interviews, SA Bank had deployed SAFe 4.5 but used only three of the four layers [8, 16]: They did not use the "large solution" layer but had the intention to deploy it in coming months.

Semi-permanent self-organizing agile development teams were put in place to support the planning, prioritization, harmonization, synchronization, development and release of the features/systems. The term "semi-permanent" is used to refer to teams being maintained as permanent as possible with the exception of changes related to turnover, punctual member swaps due to competence requirements, etc. The agile teams use many of the Scrum tools and artefacts such as backlogs, burn-down charts and Kanban walls.

5   Background Leading to the Introduction of Earn Your Wings

An incident in March 2017 triggered the introduction of the "Earn Your Wings" program. The teams were used to systematically obtain authorization to release software from a committee, composed of senior managers, called the *change advisory board* (CAB). One of the teams wanted to deploy a change into production. The changes would have been deployed using a fully automated pipeline and the team was convinced that the software would not be faulted. That release happened to occur in a high-care period. This meant that the team required authorizations from the production manager, from the business responsible, then from the area senior management head sign-off and then finally a sign-off from the CAB.

One of the people responsible for process improvement and SAFe deployment started to challenge the governance and approval process. How could they be talking about team autonomy and team self-organization while at the same time imposing a very cumbersome approval process?

After a number of focus groups, interviews and surveys, they realized that this old approval process actually had three negative side effects (what they called reverse incentive behaviors):

1. The CAB was shielding people from consequence management. If a team was deploying a change into production, so long as they received CAB sign-off, they felt relieved from taking responsibility if anything went wrong.
2. The second reverse incentive was low-low changes. Only low impact and low risk changes were self-governed. If changes were categorized as low-low, the teams did not have to go to CAB. Consequently, more and more teams were categorizing everything as low-low with the risk of deploying faulty high-risk/high-impact packages.
3. If the approval process is tedious, teams tend to package the release in larger bundles and decrease the release frequency

6   Earn Your Wings

In order to reverse these negative side effects, the team in charge of improving the deployment process at SA Bank derived a detailed evaluating and rating scheme. This section summarizes what the bank representatives presented to the researchers. They used the theme of a pilot's ability to fly an aircraft using five levels, from lowest to highest:

- **Level 1 Red Bull:** This is the lowest level for which the highest level of authorization is required. This comes from the image that "Red Bull gives you wings" but actually you are not really able to fly. In other words, the team (and the supported software) is at the lowest level of autonomy.
- **Level 2 Hot Air Balloon:** Although you can get into the air, you are reliant on fire, which can easily go up in flames. You are restricted by conditions as to whether it can take off or not. You carry very little safety gear.
- **Level 3 Small helicopter:** You have freedom of movement but with extra caution. Individually you decide if this is trusted and if the risk is worth taking. Although you can get somewhere, with relative ease, you do not have the best safety gear if something goes wrong

- **Level 4 Dinky Plane:** While you have the freedom to go wherever you want, there are situations in which you would choose not to fly. A trusted form of transport, with a little extra convincing
- **Level 5 Private Plane (highest):** Freedom to go wherever you want, whenever you want. The most trusted form of transport. Air traffic control simply coordinates but does not question.

The level is determined based on **Team Fly-ability** and **Elevation Safety** described in detail in this section.

6.1 Team Fly-Ability

Team fly-ability includes two elements "Maturity of engineering practices" (60%) and "Ability to manage traceability and risk through ease of recovery" (40%).

Maturity of Engineering Practice
The teams subjectively assess their own level of Maturity of Engineering Practices based on: the level of automation, the level of testing, the size of work package and an assessment to whether acceptance criteria are met. In practice, this is performed through a tool called *Continuum* using elements such as coding practices, continuous integration, incident management, release management, quality assurance and risk management. If teams decide to overrate themselves, they take on the risk of something going wrong.

Ease of Recovery
The ease of recovery evaluates the ability to manage traceability and risk, the time to recover and the ability to roll back and restore. This is assessed, using a tool called *Remedy,* based on the Mean Time to Recover. The objective is to maintain the down time under the agreed levels contracted in the Service Level Agreements.

6.2 Elevation Safety

Elevation Safety is based 100% on historic data on deployment performance and severity of incidents with some consideration of the application dynamics and criticality being taken into account.

Historic Data on Deployment Performance and Severity of Incidents
This is based on the performance of the previous five deployments answering questions such as: Have you caused incidents within the two weeks after your deployment due to the change? Have you had an avoidable production incident? What was the frequency of deployments?

Application Dynamics and Criticality
This is based on the chief information officer (CIO)'s list of the most critical applications with respect to: number of users, rate of change, number of dependent systems, the number of countries impacted.

6.3   Overall Assessment on a Scale of Five Levels

Using the combination of team fly-ability and elevation safety described in the previous sections, the overall level of autonomy (from Red Bull to Private Plane) is assessed using the grid in Fig. 1.

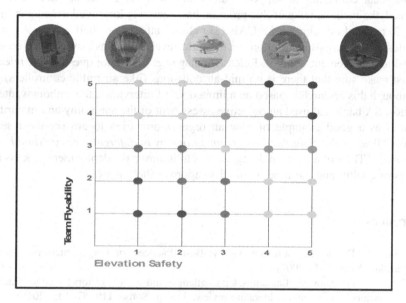

Fig. 1. Overall assessment of the team autonomy

The wings are assigned to teams, not individuals. The teams are continually assessed using real-time data (for example on the quality of their prior releases).

6.4   Authorizations Required to Deploy

The release and deployment authorizations required, depends on the level of the team as follows. This varies from required authorization of the CAB for all changes, for Level 1 (Red Bull), to complete autonomy for releasing and deployment at Level 5 (Private plane). In the case of level 5, the CAB would just be informed and would not be involved in the decision. There are various degrees of authorizations required for intermediate team level medium or above. Depending on the level, the release and deployment constraints are specified e.g. ability to release during the freeze periods, time of the day when deployment is allowed, frequency of deployment (per week), artefacts required.

7 Conclusion

At the time of the interviews, 70 teams had "earned their wings." The objective was to deploy to approximately 300 teams. Consequently, the organization was working on the improvement of engineering practices to support teams. They also continued to automate data collection to support team evaluation. As far as the SA Bank was concerned, the main benefits of this program had been: (1) Improved accountability of teams (2) reduced duration of the CAB (3) reduced attempts to find workarounds and loopholes and (4) coordination done at the right level i.e. teams govern each other as opposed to management doing it. Release management does not question the releases; they just make sure that there is no mid-air collisions (like air traffic controllers).

Although this research is based on a limited set of interviews, the authors wanted to share how SA bank had used an objective assessment of the autonomy and maturity of the teams as a good example of how an organization tried to answer the research question, *"What is the right degree of team autonomy in different contexts (and how to measure it)?"* Their objective, in doing so, was to improve the deployment process both in terms of quality and the time required to approve the releases.

References

1. Leffingwell, D.: Scaling Software Agility: Best Practices for Large Enterprises. Pearson Education, New York (2007)
2. Dikert, K., Paasivaara, M., Lassenius, C.: Challenges and success factors for large-scale agile transformations: a systematic literature review. J. Syst. Softw. **119**, 87–108 (2016)
3. Hobbs, B., Petit, Y.: Agile methods on large projects in large organizations. Proj. Manag. J. **48**(3), 3–19 (2017)
4. Ambler, S., Lines, M.: Disciplined Agile Delivery. An agile process decision framework for the enterprise (2014). http://disciplinedagiledelivery.com/
5. Vaidya, A.: Does dad know best, is it better to do less or just be safe? Adapting scaling agile practices into the enterprise. In: Pacific Northwest Software Quality Conference (PNSQC), Portland, OR (2014)
6. Mashal, A., Rozilawati, R.: A review of scaling agile methods in large software development. Int. J. Adv. Sci. **6**(6), 828–837 (2016)
7. Scaled Agile, Inc. and VersionOne present webinar on the indispensable elements of SAFe, Amman (2016)
8. Leffingwell, D.: SAFe® 40 Reference Guide: Scaled Agile Framework® for Lean Software and Systems Engineering, p. 576. Addison-Wesley Professional, Boston (2017)
9. Agile Alliance: Manifesto for Agile Software Development (2001). http://agilemanifesto. org/. Accessed 15 Jan 2013
10. Stray, V., Moe, N.B., Hoda, R.: Autonomous agile teams: challenges and future directions for research. In: Proceedings of the 19th International Conference on Agile Software Development Companion (XP 2018). ACM, New York (2018)
11. Parker, D.W., Holesgrove, M., Pathak, R.: Improving productivity with self-organised teams and agile leadership. Int. J. Prod. Perform. Manag. **64**(1), 112–128 (2015)
12. Cordery, J.L., et al.: The impact of autonomy and task uncertainty on team performance: a longitudinal field study. J. Organ. Behav. **31**(2/3), 240–258 (2010)

13. Tessem, B.: The customer effect in agile system development projects. A process tracing case study. Proc. Comput. Sci. **121**, 244–251 (2017)
14. Tripp, J.F., Riemenschneider, C., Thatcher, J.B.: Job satisfaction in agile development teams: agile development as work redesign. J. Assoc. Inf. Syst. **17**(4), 267–307 (2016)
15. Kakar, A.K.: Enhancing reflexivity in software development teams: should we focus on autonomy or interdependence? J. Inf. Technol. Theory Appl. **17**(3), 5–23 (2016)
16. Leffingwell, D.: SAFe - scaled agile framework (2015). http://www.scaledagileframework.com/. Accessed 25 Mar 2019

Open Access This chapter is licensed under the terms of the Creative Commons Attribution 4.0 International License (http://creativecommons.org/licenses/by/4.0/), which permits use, sharing, adaptation, distribution and reproduction in any medium or format, as long as you give appropriate credit to the original author(s) and the source, provide a link to the Creative Commons license and indicate if changes were made.

The images or other third party material in this chapter are included in the chapter's Creative Commons license, unless indicated otherwise in a credit line to the material. If material is not included in the chapter's Creative Commons license and your intended use is not permitted by statutory regulation or exceeds the permitted use, you will need to obtain permission directly from the copyright holder.

7th International Workshop on Large-Scale Agile

Future Trends in Agile at Scale: A Summary of the 7th International Workshop on Large-Scale Agile Development

Julian M. Bass[✉] [iD]

Computer Science and Software Engineering, University of Salford, Manchester, UK
j.bass@salford.ac.uk

Abstract. This workshop explored the main research challenges in conducting agile software development in large-scale software development. We considered multi-site companies with projects that include a large number of teams which develop sophisticated systems by adopting and using agile methods. Such topics include inter-team coordination, knowledge sharing, agile transformations, and project management models that facilitate multiple cooperating self-organising teams. The keynote talk, by Darja Šmite, provided empirical results on communities of practice within the music streaming service Spotify. We accepted five full research papers which are included in this volume. These five papers report empirical research studies using surveys, observational and case studies. Workshop participants also worked together in groups to establish current research topics and priorities. This workshop summary contributes a current snapshot of research along with future research agendas in the field of large-scale agile development.

Keywords: Large-scale agile software development · Architecture ·
Portfolio management · Project management · Scaling ·
Inter-team coordination · Software engineering · Agile transformation ·
Business agility · Knowledge sharing

1 Introduction

The goal of this workshop was to explore the main research challenges in conducting large-scale software development programmes using agile methods. We conducted a half-day workshop during the XP conference in Montréal in May 2019. How to apply agile methods to large projects was identified as the "top burning research question" by practitioners at XP2010 and has since then attracted increasing interest among practitioners and researchers. The first of this workshop series was organized at XP2013.

Agile software development methods are conventionally applied in small, co-located development teams. There is growing interest, from researchers and practitioners, in agile methods applied to large-scale projects which comprise multiple self-organising teams cooperating to develop sophisticated software systems.

© The Author(s) 2019
R. Hoda (Ed.): XP 2019 Workshops, LNBIP 364, pp. 75–80, 2019.
https://doi.org/10.1007/978-3-030-30126-2_9

This workshop addressed research challenges in large-scale agile development and identified topics such as inter-team coordination, large project organization, release planning and architecture and practices for scaling agile methods.

2 IEEE Software Special

The workshop followed a recent special issue on "Large-scale Agile" in IEEE Software [4]. The special issue, published in March/April 2019, comprised four papers. The first paper, explored the relationships between project size, agile practices, and successful software development [10]. Flexible scope, frequent deliveries to production, ability to tolerate a high degree of requirement changes and more competent providers appear to enable the success of agile approaches to development in large-scale projects.

The second paper, investigated implementing large-scale agile frameworks [3]. A fifteen year collaborative study led to the researchers identifying nine challenges to large-scale agile transformations. Among the main challenges are: top-down versus bottom-up implementation, overemphasis on 100% framework adherence over value and lack of evidence-based use.

The third paper, explored knowledge sharing in large-scale agile organizations [16]. Specifically, the guild model in the Spotify culture was examined. In Spotify, guilds are a recognised instantiation of the concept of communities of practice [19] implemented to promote collaboration among engineers across the company. This paper formed the basis of the keynote talk for the workshop reported here.

Finally, the fourth paper, investigated product owner behaviours [1]. Product owners, in Scrum terminology, identify and prioritise requirements as well as approving finished software for release. However, on large scale projects, the scope of activities required goes beyond the capacity of one person. The notions of "area product owners" [15] or product owner teams [2] have previously been explored. The current study found that face-to-face interactions are preferred, when dealing with geographical, temporal, and cultural distances [1]. On projects regarded by practitioners as successful, product owners use their influencing skills to keep a wide range of stakeholders focused on a specific set of goals. Experienced product owners use a minimum viable product to create the capacity for change. The study suggests that the process of building a product owner team should be explicit and well defined.

3 Workshop Contributions

The workshop comprised a keynote talk, speakers selected following submission of short papers, which were peer-reviewed by members of the program committee, and an interactive session to identify research topics and priorities.

3.1   Keynote

The keynote talk, by Prof. Darja Ŝmite from Blekinge Institute of Technology in Sweden [17], focused on Guild use within Spotify, the internet music streaming service, and was based on the recent article in IEEE Software [16]. Guilds are a social structure for stewarding knowledge or an explicit way to inculcate communities of practice within the organisation. The research found that engagement in guilds, at Spotify, is cultivated through annual un-conferences, "Slack" channels and electronically-mediated opinion elicitation (requests for comments).

3.2   Research Papers

For the 2019 workshop we had seven submissions, of which five were accepted as full research paper presentations. The first paper "SAFe Adoptions in Finland: A Survey Research" reported benefits in terms of transparency, co-operation and cadence [12]. However, organisations adopting SAFe reported challenges with legacy organisational structures, lack of tailoring to their context and implementation issues. The respondents reported that SAFe was being used in conjunction with other agile practices. The authors also observed evidence of incomplete adoption of SAFe practices.

The second paper, "Comparing Scaling Agile Frameworks Based on Underlying Practices" identifies several common practices among adopters of scaled agile frameworks [18]. The authors found that many scrum project and scaling practices underpin the frameworks observed in their study. The authors present an interesting "subway map" diagram to illustrate practices used in several frameworks as compared with more esoteric practices.

The third paper, "Finnish Large-Scale Agile Transformations: A Survey Study" is based on the same survey as the first paper [11]. In this third paper, the authors found that 44% of their survey respondents have completed an agile transformation at least one year prior to the survey. A further 30% of the respondents in the study are in the process of an agile transformation. The authors also discovered that 60% of the respondents in the study worked in organisations that made use of external consultants or subcontractors in order to assist the change process. The authors suggest that organisations use consultants and subcontractors to provide new competencies and additional resources to perform transformations.

The forth paper, "Changes Over Time in a Planned Inter-Team Coordination Routine" investigates the Programme Increment (PI) Planning routine [9]. PI Planning is considered a fundamental practice within SAFe. The author conducted an observational study of PI Planning within three organisations and found differences in the approaches being taken. This study suggests that organisations are tailoring their SAFe PI Planning practices.

Finally, the fifth paper "Technical-, Social- and Process Debt in Large-Scale Agile: an exploratory case-study" explores how using short-term expedient technical or organisational constructs can make future change more difficult or expensive [13]. The research reveals that process debt is resolved by inter-team coordination, and that teams spend a lot of time discussing social debt in retrospectives.

3.3   Future Research Trends

The workshop attendees were asked to work in four groups, each group addressing one topic adapted from research priorities identified during the 2017 workshop [14]. Thus, the four groups were considering:

- Inter-team Communication,
- Agile Transformation, Business Agility,
- Knowledge Sharing, Knowledge Networks, and
- Scaling Agile.

Each of the four groups considered important issues in each of the topics. Each group was then asked to prioritise the topics. The results of each group is presented as a flip chart illustration, available online as follows:

- Inter-team Communication [5],
- Agile Transformation, Business Agility [6],
- Knowledge Sharing, Knowledge Networks [7], and
- Scaling Agile [8].

For inter-team coordination, the group emphasised the continuum of team alignment to strategy and autonomy along with new roles and new communication modes enabled by new tools. For agile transformation and business agility, the group emphasised issues around measurement, budgeting and success as well as customer collaboration and agile framework evaluation. For knowledge sharing and knowledge networks, the group emphasised on-boarding new team members, finding competencies in the organisation and balancing knowledge sharing with focused work. Finally, for scaling agile the group emphasised public sector agile along with "how is agile visible (in mindset and results) to senior executives?" as well as issues of trust and transparency.

4   Programme Committee

Many thanks to the members of the programme committee many of whom have also contributed to previous workshops, as follows:

- Steve Adolph, cPrime, Canada
- Finn Olav Bjornson, NTNU, Norway
- Torgeir Dingsøyr, Sintef, Norway
- Jutta Eckstein, IT Communication, Germany
- Peggy Gregory, UCLAN, UK
- Tomas Gustavsson, Karlstad University, Sweden
- Andy Haxby, Competa, Netherlands
- Aymeric Hemon, Université de Nantes, France
- Eric Knauss, Gothenburg University, Sweden
- Maarit Laanti, Nitor, Finland
- Carl Marnewick, University of Johannesburg, South Africa

- Nils Brede Moe, Sintef, Norway
- Helena Holmstrom Olsson, Malmö University, Sweden
- Maria Paasivaara, Aalto University, Finland
- Yvan Petit, ESG UQAM, Canada
- Alexander Poth, Volkswagen, Germany
- Ken Power, Cisco, Ireland
- Klaas-Jan Stol, Lero, Ireland

Without the valuable support of these programme committee members the workshop would not have been possible. Thanks also to Rashina Hoda, the Workshop Chair for XP 2019, who enabled the workshop within the XP conference framework.

5 Conclusions

This workshop successfully created an opportunity for researchers and practitioners to consider the latest trends in large-scale agile development. The papers in these proceedings, the keynote and interactive session contribute a snapshot of the start-of-the-art in this field. The authors presented evidence of frameworks being used to enable agile transformations in organisations, but also of incomplete adoption of frameworks and commonalities between practices being used in frameworks.

References

1. Bass, J.M., Haxby, A.: Tailoring product ownership in large-scale agile projects: managing scale, distance, and governance. IEEE Softw. **36**(2), 58–63 (2019). https://doi.org/10.1109/MS.2018.2885524
2. Bass, J.M.: How product owner teams scale agile methods to large distributed enterprises. Empir. Softw. Eng. **20**(6), 1525–1557 (2015). https://doi.org/10.1007/s10664-014-9322-z
3. Conboy, K., Carroll, N.: Implementing large-scale agile frameworks: challenges and recommendations. IEEE Softw. **36**(2), 44–50 (2019). https://doi.org/10.1109/MS.2018.2884865
4. Dingsoeyr, T., Falessi, D., Power, K.: Agile development at scale: the next frontier. IEEE Softw. **36**(2), 30–38 (2019). https://doi.org/10.1109/MS.2018.2884884
5. Group 1: Inter-team communication, June 2019. https://doi.org/10.17866/rd.salford.8320193, https://salford.figshare.com/articles/Group_1_Inter-team_Communication/8320193/0
6. Group 2: Agile transformation, business agility, June 2019. https://doi.org/10.17866/rd.salford.8320184, https://salford.figshare.com/articles/Group_2_Agile_Transformation_Business_Agility/8320184/0
7. Group 3: Knowledge sharing, knowledge networks, June 2019. https://doi.org/10.17866/rd.salford.8320175, https://salford.figshare.com/articles/Group_3_Knowledge_Sharing_Knowledge_Networks/8320175/0
8. Group 4: Scaling agile, June 2019. https://doi.org/10.17866/rd.salford.8320172, https://salford.figshare.com/articles/Group_4_Scaling_Agile/8320172/0

9. Gustavsson, T.: Changes over time in a planned inter-team coordination routine. In: Hoda, R. (ed.) XP 2019 Workshops. LNBIP, vol. 364, pp. 105–111. Springer, Cham (2019)

10. Jorgensen, M.: Relationships between project size, agile practices, and successful software development: results and analysis. IEEE Softw. **36**(2), 39–43 (2019). https://doi.org/10.1109/MS.2018.2884863

11. Kuttenen, P., Laanti, M., Fagerholm, F., Mikkonen, T., Männistö, T.: Finnish enterprise agile transformations: a survey study. In: Hoda, R. (ed.) XP 2019 Workshops. LNBIP, vol. 364, pp. 97–104. Springer, Cham (2019)

12. Laanti, M., Kuttenen, P.: SAFe adoptions in Finland: a survey research. In: Hoda, R. (ed.) XP 2019 Workshops. LNBIP, vol. 364, pp. 81–87. Springer, Cham (2019)

13. Martini, A., Stray, V., Brede Moe, N.: Technical-, social- and process debt in large-scale agile: an exploratory case-study. In: Hoda, R. (ed.) XP 2019 Workshops. LNBIP, vol. 364, pp. 112–119. Springer, Cham (2019)

14. Moe, N.B., Dingsøyr, T.: Emerging research themes and updated research agenda for large-scale agile development: a summary of the 5th international workshop at XP 2017. In: Proceedings of the XP 2017 Scientific Workshops, XP 2017, pp. 14:1–14:4. ACM (2017). https://doi.org/10.1145/3120459.3120474

15. Paasivaara, M., Heikkilä, V.T., Lassenius, C.: Experiences in scaling the product owner role in large-scale globally distributed scrum. In: 2012 IEEE Seventh International Conference on Global Software Engineering, pp. 174–178, August 2012. https://doi.org/10.1109/ICGSE.2012.41

16. Smite, D., Moe, N.B., Levinta, G., Floryan, M.: Spotify guilds: how to succeed with knowledge sharing in large-scale agile organizations. IEEE Softw. **36**(2), 51–57 (2019). https://doi.org/10.1109/MS.2018.2886178

17. Šmite, D.: Scaling parallel structures: the spotify guilds' story, May 2019. https://static.sched.com/hosted_files/xp2019/9b/Darja%20Smite_%20Keynote.pdf

18. Theobald, S., Schmitt, A., Diebold, P.: Comparing scaling agile frameworks based on underlying practices. In: Hoda, R. (ed.) XP 2019 Workshops. LNBIP, vol. 364, pp. 88–96. Springer, Cham (2019)

19. Wenger, E., McDermott, R., Snyder, W.: Cultivating Communities of Practice: A Guide to Managing Knowledge. Harvard Business School Press, Boston (2002)

Open Access This chapter is licensed under the terms of the Creative Commons Attribution 4.0 International License (http://creativecommons.org/licenses/by/4.0/), which permits use, sharing, adaptation, distribution and reproduction in any medium or format, as long as you give appropriate credit to the original author(s) and the source, provide a link to the Creative Commons license and indicate if changes were made.

The images or other third party material in this chapter are included in the chapter's Creative Commons license, unless indicated otherwise in a credit line to the material. If material is not included in the chapter's Creative Commons license and your intended use is not permitted by statutory regulation or exceeds the permitted use, you will need to obtain permission directly from the copyright holder.

SAFe Adoptions in Finland: A Survey Research

Maarit Laanti[1(✉)] and Petri Kettunen[2]

[1] Nitor Delta, Helsinki, Finland
`maarit.laanti@nitor.com`
[2] Department of Computer Science, University of Helsinki, Helsinki, Finland
`petri.kettunen@helsinki.fi`

Abstract. Scaled Agile Framework (SAFe) was released in the year 2011. Since then it has become the most popular agile scaling framework in use. In this paper we examine the benefits and obstacles of SAFe adoptions in Finland. The data is based on a survey we conducted in Finland in 2018, when many respondents had already been following SAFe for some years. The biggest benefits reported are transparency, co-operation, and cadence. The biggest obstacles are the old organizational culture, that the SAFe model has not been fitted to the organization and implementation problems. The results indicate that although many respondents of the survey (80%) use SAFe, they are still struggling with their agile transformation, while using a mix of old and new methods and only a subset of the SAFe practices.

Keywords: Scaled Agile Framework · SAFe · Agile transformation · Large-scale agile · Scaled Agile · Agile

1 Introduction and Background

Scaled Agile Framework (SAFe) was launched in the 2011 Agile conference [1]. Since then it has become the dominant agile scaling model in large enterprises [2]. According to the 12th State of Agile Report conducted by Version One and Collabnet, SAFe is now the most widely adopted large-scale agile framework with the usage rate of 29% [3]. Scaled Agile Inc. has announced that there are 300,000 SAFe-certified practitioners in 110 countries, and that 70% of Fortune 100 companies employ SAFe-certified professionals [4].

Both benefits and challenges of SAFe adoptions have been reported. However, more empirical research is needed to understand how to adopt established frameworks like SAFe, how are they used and tailored, and what their benefits and challenges are under different circumstances [5, 6]. This paper examines SAFe usage, benefits, and obstacles in organizations in Finland to contribute to those research gaps.

In general industrial experiences report a 10–50% improvement in employee motivation, 30–75% faster time-to-market, 20–50% increase in productivity, and 25–75% reduction in defects [4] – but empirical research validating these results are missing. In 2017 the Large-Scale Agile Workshop called for more research on scaling agile along with inter-team coordination, knowledge sharing and knowledge networks,

© The Author(s) 2019
R. Hoda (Ed.): XP 2019 Workshops, LNBIP 364, pp. 81–87, 2019.
https://doi.org/10.1007/978-3-030-30126-2_10

agile transformation and business agility [5]. This raises numerous questions, like is SAFe used alone, or together with other agile methods? What kind of results do the companies get with it?

The existing research on SAFe cover for example SAFe and Portfolio Management [7–9], SAFe and testing [10], SAFe in distributed settings [11], maturity model for adoptions [12–14], principles of large-scale agile [15], case studies of adoption [16, 17], comparison of different scaling frameworks [18], and reported benefits and challenges [6]. However, there is lack of empirical research on SAFe adoptions and usage in companies. With this paper we are aiming to fill in the gap with a survey research into SAFe adoption across multiple industries and companies.

2   Survey Research Design

The purpose of our survey research was to examine the current state of Agile in Finland. Agile has previously been surveyed in many different investigations, but currently in particular the rapid advances of digitalization make it especially topical for different organizations – not limited to software companies.

Our questionnaire was composed starting from our selected main themes of interests including SAFe usage and transformations. The specific questions were then compiled by referring to prior surveys for comparison purposes (e.g., [20]) and by deriving from our industrial experiences. The target audience was intentionally not limited to software companies since we were also interested in non-software companies currently facing digitalization and becoming more software-intensive. The draft questionnaire was first piloted both in our industrial and academic organizations. The final version consisted of 50 questions with some variable parts depending on the selector questions. Especially the questions "What have been the three most significant benefits of the SAFe adoption?" and "What have been the three biggest obstacles to the SAFe transformation (adoption)?" were only presented to those respondents who stated they are using SAFe.

The survey was implemented as a web-based online questionnaire. The questionnaire was distributed social media and a proprietary industrial mailing list mass postings to over 600 people, and it was open for responding for four weeks during November and December in 2018.

3   Results

We received 136 responses to our survey, out of which 111 respondents (80%) were using SAFe. In this paper "SAFe users" refer to all respondents that replied to the multi choice question "What agile methods and models are there in use in Your company?" with the choice 'Scaled Agile Framework (SAFe)'. Part of this group also used Scrum and Kanban and other methods. "Non-SAFe users" refer to the respondents stating they were not using SAFe. This is because the aim was to study differences between these two groups. Also there was no significant difference detected what comes to the length of agile methods adoption between SAFe and non-SAFe users.

The majority of respondents were using agile methods ("How widely does Your company use agile methods in software development?") either for their entire organization (20%) or for the entire business unit (59%); see Fig. 1. The result is in line with SAFe targeted to be the operational model for the entire company. Yet the further analysis of results reveals that there is no significant difference between SAFe users and non-SAFe users in this respect. In fact, it seems that many respondents use multiple methods mixed together. 90% of all SAFe users used also Scrum, and 83% Kanban, 12% XP, 12% own model, 9% LeSS and 2% DAD. Only 5% of all SAFe users (6 respondents) responded that SAFe is the only agile method they use.

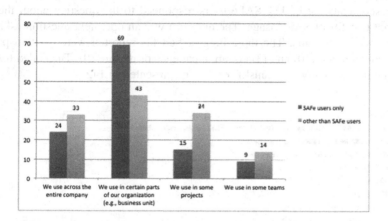

Fig. 1. Most respondents use agile methods in entire company or in parts of the organization. Legend shows number of respondents (multiple choices allowed).

Figure 2 presents the SAFe practices the respondents use. Not all respondents responded to this free text question.

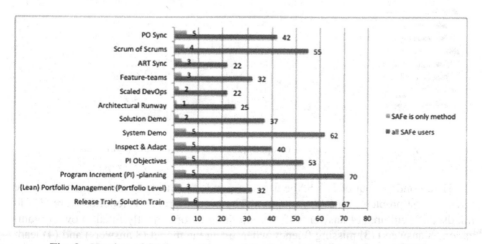

Fig. 2. Number of SAFe practices used by those respondents who use SAFe.

With the scale from 0–100 most of the respondents (96 replies) thought that SAFe as useful, with the average of 65,78; see Table 1.

Table 1. Statistical analysis of the responses to the question about the usefulness of SAFe with the scale from 0–100.

N	EOS	X	STDEV X	ERROR X	95% INTERVAL
96	9	65,78	20,68	2,22	61,44-70,13

47 respondents out of 111 SAFe users responded to the question about the most significant benefits of SAFe usage. The question was an open text question asking for the three biggest benefits. The three biggest benefits reported were (1) transparency (24) (2) co-operation (10) and (3) common cadence or rhythm (9). The coded (original answering data partially in Finnish) results are presented in Fig. 4.

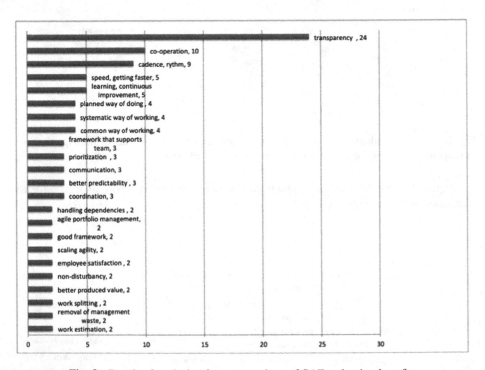

Fig. 3. Result of analysis of open questions of SAFe adoption benefits.

51 respondents out of 111 SAFe users responded to the open text question to name three biggest problems on SAFe adoption. The biggest problems reported were (1) old mindset and culture (14 answers), (2) the model has not correctly fitted to own organization (8 answers) (3) missing fluency when using the model (8 answers) and (4) leadership (7 answers). Figure 3 represents a coding summary of these open answers.

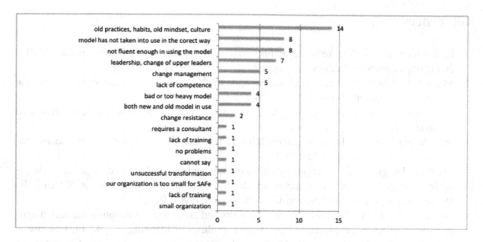

Fig. 4. Answers to three biggest problems in SAFe adoption analyzed.

4   Discussion and Conclusion

The purpose of our research was to study the state of SAFe adoption in companies in Finland. Yet, because of the anonymous nature of the survey we do not know exactly how many companies were represented by these answers. The respondents represented widely different industries though, and not just software or IT industries.

The results indicate that although SAFe is widely in use (80% respondents), it has not in most cases replaced other methods and old practices, but is used together with those methods and practices. Only 5% of respondents stated that they are using SAFe as the only method. Most likely these could be e.g. subcontractors that work only with SAFe. The most commonly received benefit received with SAFe is transparency. The conclusion is, that although methodologist discuss hectically of the pros and cons of different models, most organizations use a combination of these methods.

Transparency is usually just the first benefit of SAFe transformation that is received when organizations have implemented backlogs. SAFe is also being used without using all the SAFe practices; e.g. only 20% replied that they use DevOps with SAFe. We though received feedback that the term Scaled DevOps used specifically as the choice in this question caused confusion amongst the respondents – thus the real number of DevOps users could be higher than indicated by responses.

The conclusion is that although many respondents stated they were using SAFe, it seems that most organizations are still at the beginning of their agile transformation. The benefits that SAFe lists got also mentioned but less often (see Fig. 4): execution speed was 4th mentioned benefit (5 notes) Value and employee satisfaction were both mentioned only 2 times, but improved quality was not listed as a benefit.

We hope to conduct a longitudinal study in this area and see if the responses change over time. We also hope to get more results on what are the reasons behind successful and non-successful agile transformations. We also hope that we can repeat a similar study in Sweden and compare those results to these in Finland reported here.

References

1. Leffingwell, D.: Scaling software agility: advanced practices for large enterprise. AGILE 2011. https://www.agilealliance.org/agile2011/. Accessed 11 June 2019
2. Mashal, A., Razali, R.: A review of scaling agile methods in large software development. Int. J. Adv. Sci. Eng. Inf. Technol. 6(6), 828–837 (2016)
3. Version one (12th) annual state of agile report. https://stateofagile.versionone.com. Accessed 11 June 2019
4. Introducing SAFe for lean companies. https://www.scaledagileframework.com/videos-and-presentations/. Accessed 11 June 2019
5. Moe, N., Dingsøyr, T.: Emerging research themes and updated research agenda for large-scale agile development: a summary of the 5th international workshop at XP2017. In: Proceedings of the XP2017 Scientific Workshops. ACM (2017)
6. Putta, A., Paasivaara, M., Lassenius, C.: Benefits and challenges of adopting the scaled agile framework (SAFe): preliminary results from a multivocal literature review. In: Kuhrmann, M., et al. (eds.) PROFES 2018. LNCS, vol. 11271, pp. 334–351. Springer, Cham (2018). https://doi.org/10.1007/978-3-030-03673-7_24
7. Stettina, C., Hörz, J.: Agile portfolio management: an empirical perspective on the practice in use. Int. J. Project Manag. 33(1), 140–152 (2015)
8. Laanti, M., Sirkiä, R., Kangas, M.: Agile portfolio management at Finnish Broadcasting Company Yle. In: Scientific Workshop Proceedings of the XP2015 (XP '15 workshops), p. 7. ACM, New York (2015). Article 1
9. Laanti, M., Kangas, M.: Is agile portfolio management following the principles of large-scale agile? Case study in Finnish Broadcasting Company Yle. In: 2015 Agile Conference, Washington, DC, pp. 92–96 (2015)
10. Fridälv, S.: Evaluating the implementation of SAFe with focus on test and quality. LU-CS-EX 2017–02 (2017)
11. Paasivaara, M.: Adopting SAFe to scale agile in a globally distributed organization. In: ICGSE, IEEE 12th International Conference on Global Software Engineering (2017)
12. Turetken, O., Stojanov, I., Trienekens, J.J.M.: Assessing the adoption level of scaled agile development: a maturity model for scaled agile framework. J. Softw. Evol. Proc. 29, e1796 (2017)
13. Stojanov, I., Turetken, O., Trienekens, J.: A maturity model for scaling agile development. In: 41st Euromicro Conference on Software Engineering and Advanced Applications (2015)
14. Laanti, M.: Agile transformation model for large software development organizations. In: Proceedings of the XP2017 Scientific Workshops. ACM (2017)
15. Laanti, M.: Characteristics and principles of scaled agile. In: Dingsøyr, T., Moe, N.B., Tonelli, R., Counsell, S., Gencel, C., Petersen, K. (eds.) XP 2014. LNBIP, vol. 199, pp. 9–20. Springer, Cham (2014). https://doi.org/10.1007/978-3-319-14358-3_2
16. Brenner, R., Wunder, S.: Scaled agile framework: presentation and real world example. In: IEEE Eighth International Conference on Software Testing, Verification and Validation Workshops (ICSTW), Graz, pp. 1–2 (2015)
17. Dikert, K., Paasivaara, M., Lassenius, C.: Challenges and success factors for large-scale agile transformations: a systematic literature review. J. Syst. Softw. 119, 87–108 (2016)
18. Laanti, M.: Agile methods in large-scale software development organizations – applicability and model for adoption. Dissertation, Oulu University (2013)
19. Ebert, C., Paasivaara, M.: Scaling agile. IEEE Softw. 34(6), 98–103 (2017)
20. Finnish Software Industry Survey. http://www.softwareindustrysurvey.fi/focus-on-flexibility-agility-in-software-development/. Accessed 11 June 2019

Open Access This chapter is licensed under the terms of the Creative Commons Attribution 4.0 International License (http://creativecommons.org/licenses/by/4.0/), which permits use, sharing, adaptation, distribution and reproduction in any medium or format, as long as you give appropriate credit to the original author(s) and the source, provide a link to the Creative Commons license and indicate if changes were made.

The images or other third party material in this chapter are included in the chapter's Creative Commons license, unless indicated otherwise in a credit line to the material. If material is not included in the chapter's Creative Commons license and your intended use is not permitted by statutory regulation or exceeds the permitted use, you will need to obtain permission directly from the copyright holder.

Comparing Scaling Agile Frameworks Based on Underlying Practices

Sven Theobald[1]([✉]) [iD], Anna Schmitt[1] [iD], and Philipp Diebold[2] [iD]

[1] Fraunhofer IESE, Fraunhofer-Platz 1, 67663 Kaiserslautern, Germany
{sven.theobald,Anna.schmitt}@iese.fraunhofer.de
[2] Bagilstein GmbH, Mainz, Germany
philipp.diebold@bagilstein.de

Abstract. *Context*: Agile software development is widely-used by small teams and has benefits like increased transparency or faster feedback. However, companies want to benefit from Agile also in the development of big products, where multiple teams are involved. Many Scaling Agile Frameworks exist, but only few can be found in industry, especially SAFe, LeSS, and Nexus. *Objective*: The aim of this work is to identify commonalities of existing Scaling Agile Frameworks concerning their practices. *Method*: We extracted and consolidated the practices of twelve frameworks and compared the frameworks based on their practices using a visualization. *Results*: Frameworks prescribe scaling practices as well as practices on team level. There are practices common to most frameworks like the scaled Scrum events, e.g., a scaled planning meeting or retrospective. *Conclusion*: Practitioners are enabled to make informed decisions when choosing or tailoring their individual Scaling Agile Framework.

Keywords: Agile development · Scaling agile · Scaling frameworks · Scaling practices · Framework comparison · Subway Map

1 Introduction

The rising popularity of agile software development is based on many benefits like managing changing priorities, increasing time to market or team moral [1]. Agile is composed of values, principles, and methods. Scrum [2] is the most used agile method across all organization types and sizes [1]. All these methods base on different Agile Practices, like Daily Stand-Up or Sprint [2]. However, Scrum and all other Agile Methods are not sufficient to achieve the desired benefits of all kinds of organizations regarding agile development. Especially for big projects or organizations, Agile Methods are not sufficient, since they were designed for small teams only. However, organizations with big teams also want to develop Agile. Therefore, several so-called Scaling Agile Frameworks increasingly came up in the last six years. The most famous ones according to [1] are the Scaled Agile Framework (SAFe) [3] and Scrum-of-Scrums [4]. For those commonly used frameworks, some experience reports and studies exist, especially for SAFe [4–6]. However, also less known ones like FAST Agile Scaled Technology (FAST) [7] or Recipes for Agile Governance (RAGE) [8]

© The Author(s) 2019
R. Hoda (Ed.): XP 2019 Workshops, LNBIP 364, pp. 88–96, 2019.
https://doi.org/10.1007/978-3-030-30126-2_11

exist. Scaling frameworks are based on practices on the technological and managerial level. These practices form the foundation for the implementation of all frameworks. Only [9] conducted a comparison on practice level so far and identified eight common scaling practices by comparing LeSS and SAFe. If Scaling Agile Frameworks were compared directly in related work, the comparison was along characteristics of the frameworks [10–12]. [13] compared eight Scaling Agile Frameworks on how IT governance is covered. In this work, we aim to identify the commonalities of Scaling Agile Frameworks concerning their defined practices. We used the twelve Scaling Agile Frameworks from [12] and updated the visualization [12]. To be able to conduct a comparison on practice level, we first extracted and consolidated all practices from these twelve Scaling Agile Frameworks.

2 Overview Over Practices

We went through the descriptions of each practice given by the frameworks. Based on these descriptions, we divided the practices into three groups: (1) practices that are only used on team level (cf. Table 1 that only displays the Scrum practices), (2) practices that are only used to scale agile (c.f. Table 2), and (3) practices that can be used for both – scaling agile and on team level (c.f. Table 3). Based on this classification, we created three different tables that provide an overview of the categories, subcategories, and related practices. Scaling Agile frameworks do not only define scaling practices, but also demand practices on team level. These coordination mechanisms for each team help to better align multiple teams. Table 1 only shows the Scrum practices, since they also appear in the Subway Map. Scrum is the most commonly used method [1]. It describes the management practices without prescribing technical practices [14]. Most scaling frameworks base on Scrum on team level.

Table 1. Scrum practices used on team level

Categories	Subcategories	Practices
Meeting types	Daily Stand-Up	Daily Scrum, Daily Stand-Up, Weekly Scrum, Stand-Up Meeting, Daily Coordination Meeting
Planning Meeting	Sprint Planning	Iteration Planning, Sprint Planning Part 1, Sprint Planning and Investigation, Phase Planning, Sprint Planning, Planning Session, FAST Meeting - Part 2: Marketplace in Open Space style, Kick-Off
Backlog Preparation	Product Backlog	Backlog, Product Backlog, Tribe Product Backlog, Team Backlog
	Sprint Backlog	Sprint Backlog, Iteration Backlog
	Backlog Refinement	Backlog Grooming, Product Backlog Refinement, Backlog Decomposition, Backlog Prioritization, PBI Inspection (in Sprint), Look-ahead Planning

(continued)

Table 1. (*continued*)

Categories	Subcategories	Practices
Iterative Procedure	*Sprint*	Sprint, Synchronous Sprints, Iteration
Lessons Learned	*Retrospective*	Retrospective, Sprint Retrospective, Iteration Retrospective, Team Retrospective
Review/Demo	*Review/Demo*	Sprint Review, Sprint Review Record, Iteration Review, Production Readiness Review, Light-Weight Milestone Review, FAST-Meeting - Part 1: Review (show and tell), Project Review
Progress Activities	*Definition of Done*	Definition of Done

On a scaled level (cf. Table 2), many practices on team level are adapted on a scaled level. Team level practices like the Scrum events were adapted for a scaled environment, e.g. by changing the participants of the events. Many frameworks also demand team level mechanisms, such as a Kanban board, Burn Charts or Release Planning activities, to be used in scaled projects. In addition, dedicated scaling practices like the Architecture Release Train from SAFe help to align the work of teams.

Table 2. Scaling practices

Categories	Subcategories	Practices
Meeting Types	*Scrum-of-Scrums*	Scrum-of-Scrums-Meeting, Scrum-of-Scrums, Nexus Daily Scrum, Cross-Team Coordination, Inter-Team Coordination Meeting
	Product Owner Sync	Product Owner Sync
Planning Meeting	*Scaled Planning*	Program Increment Planning, Sprint Planning Part 2, Nexus Sprint Planning, Portfolio Planning Meeting, Multisite Sprint Planning Part 1
	Scaled (Sprint) Goal	FAST Meeting - Part III: Announcements and Alignment of Vision, Nexus Sprint Goal, Program Increment Objective, Terms of Reference, Agile Charter
Backlog Preparation	*Scaled Backlog*	Program Backlog, Sync Backlog, Portfolio Backlog, Nexus Sprint Backlog
	Scaled Backlog Refinement	Joint Light Product Backlog Refinement, Multisite Product Backlog Refinement, Portfolio Grooming Meeting

(*continued*)

Table 2. (*continued*)

Categories	Subcategories	Practices
Manage Impediments	*Scaling Impediments Management*	Impediments (Backlog)
Delivery	*Agile Release Train*	Agile Release Train, Release Train
Architecture	*Architectural Runway*	Architectural Runway
Open Source Data	*Collective Ownership*	Collective Ownership
Release Activities	*Release Planning*	Release Planning, Release Management, Release Planning Meeting
	Release Handoffs	Release Handoffs
	Release Review	Release Review
Lessons Learned	*Scaled Retrospective*	Joint Retrospective, Nexus Sprint Retrospective, Inspect & Adapt Workshop
Review/Demo	*Review/Demo*	Quality Assessment
	Scaled Review	Overall Sprint Review, Multisite Sprint Review, Staging Readiness Review, Nexus Sprint Review, System Demo
Progress Activities	*Portfolio/Program Kanban Board*	Portfolio Kanban, Program Kanban
Others		*Initiative Assessment, Flex-Teaming, Beta Codex, Automated Metrics*

With Table 3, we show that there are also practices that are demanded on team level, but are also demanded under scaling conditions. This does not necessarily mean that the same framework demands a practice in both environments; it could also be that one framework uses the practice on team level, whereas another framework uses the practice as a scaling mechanism. General concepts like Time Boxing, Estimation or Open Source can be used by a single team as well as by multiple teams. User Stories help to describe the functionality of a product, independent of how many teams are responsible for this product. Communities of Practice are independent from projects. There are also practices that gain importance in a scaled environment, like Architecture or Release Activities. A focus on such topics is essential due to the increased coordination effort of multiple teams and the complexity of larger products. Likewise, Strategic Activities that can also already be applied on team level, support alignment of teams and reduce risk related to larger complex products.

Table 3. Practices for both scaled and team level

Categories	Subcategories	Practices
Meeting Types	Timeboxing	Timeboxing
Planning Meeting	Prioritization	Prioritization Meeting, MoSCoW, Prioritized Requirements List
Backlog Preparation	Transition Backlog	Evaluation Backlog, Transition Backlog, Practice Backlog
	Release Map	Release Map
Manage Impediments	Manage Impediments	Impediment Removal, Impediment Backlog, Continuous Impediment Removal
Requirements Documentation		User Stories, Portfolio Epic, Epic, Story Document, Requirement Document
Community of Practice		Community of Practice
Iterative Procedure	Increment	Increment of Change, Integrated Increment, Evolutionary Development, Pre-and Post-Program Increment
Architecture	Architectural Envisioning	Architectural Envisioning
Open Source Data	Internal Open Source	Internal Open Source
Release Activities	Delivery/Release Plan	Delivery/Release Plan
Strategic Activities		Decision making Framework, Lean-Agile Budgeting, Value Stream, Roadmap, Strategic Themes, Business Case, Decision Matrix, Funding Decision, Project Map
Estimation		Estimation, Forecasting
Others		Benefits Assessment

3   Comparison of Frameworks

We extended our "Subway Map" inspired visualization (similar to [15]) from [12] to show (1) which framework contains which practices as well as (2) which common practices are shared by multiple frameworks (cf. Figure 1). In the Subway Map (cf. Figure 1), each line represents a Scaling Agile Framework. The single subway stations illustrate the single practices that appear in those Scaling Agile Frameworks. We wanted the comparison to be easy to understand and visible at a glance. For the sake of simplicity, some subway stations represent only categories instead of single practices. The big stations symbolize practices that are used by many frameworks, e.g. Daily Stand-Up or Product Backlog.

The Subway Map shows that some frameworks share common Scaling Practices like the scaled form of the Scrum practices, namely: Scaled (Sprint) Goal, Scaled Retrospective, Scaled Planning, Scaled Review, Scrum of Scrums, and Scaled Backlog. Whereas, some more individual practices only occur in few frameworks, such as,

Release Review, Program-/Portfolio Kanban Board, Agile Release Train, Beta Codex, and Architectural Runway. On a closer inspection, it can be seen that most of the widespread practices are based on Scrum. This can be explained by the fact that Scrum contains management practices that mainly serve to organize the process around the software development in a lightweight manner.

Table 4. Practices and their occurrence over frameworks

#	Practice	#	Practice	#	Practice
11	Sprint Planning	4	Increment	1	Manage Impediments
11	Sprint	4	Scaled Review	1	Scaling Impediments Management
10	Retrospective	4	Strategic Activities	1	Architectural Runway
10	Review/"Demo"	4	Estimation	1	Architecture Envisioning
9	Daily Stand-Up	3	Agile Release Train	1	Internal Open Source
8	Product Backlog	3	Release Planning	1	Delivery/Release Plan
7	Definition of Done	3	Scaled Retrospective	1	Release Handoffs
6	Scrum of Scrums	2	Prioritization	1	Product Deploy Validation
6	Sprint Backlog	2	Transition Backlog	1	Release Review
6	Backlog Refinement	2	Scaled Backlog Refinement	1	Beta Codex
5	Scaled Planning	2	Collective Ownership	1	Facilitated Workshop
5	Scaled (Sprint) Goal	2	Portfolio/Program Kanban Board	1	Flex-Teaming
5	Requirements Documentation	1	Product Owner Sync	1	Initiative Assessment
4	Scaled Backlog	1	Timeboxing	1	Benefits Assessment
4	Community of Practice	1	Release Map		

Technical practices like Pair Programming are rather seldom part of scaling frameworks, since they often do not scale beyond software development on team level. Furthermore, it can be seen that all Scaling Agile Frameworks include scaling practices, but also non-scaling practices, namely practices on team level. Table 4 lists the practices across the frameworks ordered by occurrence. With the help of Table 4 and our visualization, it also can be seen that the Scrum practices, which are only used on team level, are still applied by almost every framework. This obvious commonality across the frameworks was the reason to include the Scrum practices in the visualization, though they are team level practices. Sprints and sprint planning are the practices recommended by almost all frameworks.

4 Implications

If practitioners have to decide on a suitable Scaling Agile Framework, they first need to know what frameworks exist. With the list of frameworks that are considered in our comparison, practitioners understand that there are more possibilities than the well-known frameworks that are typically presented by consultants. To identify the most suitable framework, we already presented a comparison of those frameworks in previous work [12] that compares criteria like the purpose, advantages or context of those frameworks. With an initial selection of a suitable framework, it can then be extended or adapted to the specific needs, leading to an individual approach.

When designing a scaling approach, practitioners might want to check for coverage of the suggested categories of practices (cf. Tables 1, 2 and 3). The practices from those categories might be important to consider since the authors of those scaling frameworks considered them. The Subway Map provides an overview over the existing Scaling Agile Frameworks, and shows the corresponding scaling practices. It can be seen that some frameworks are rather similar, sharing many practices, while others are rather individual and provide many practices that are not covered in other frameworks. We recommend considering the most commonly used practices (cf. Table 4) first, in order to implement the best practices of multiple frameworks. In addition, the individual practices can be evaluated to complement the base framework. Our comparison of frameworks shows that many frameworks are based on Scrum on team level. Practitioners that want to scale up their agile development should first consider their implementation of team level practices that support scaled agile development.

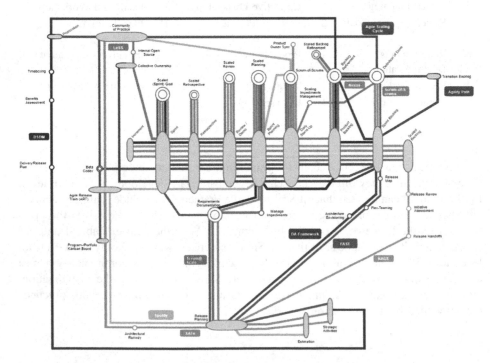

Fig. 1. Subway map visualizing practices of Scaling Agile Frameworks

The categorization of scaling practices and the Subway map need to be validated by the respective framework experts. Due to lack of documentation, there is the risk that wrong categorizations were made or practices from frameworks are missing. Since we did not conduct a systematic literature review, it might be that some frameworks or some of their practices are missing. For the sake of simplicity of the categorization, sometimes practices were clustered without considering the detailed differences. The stations of the Subway map have different abstraction levels, since some stations are based on practices, others on categories.

5   Conclusion

Due to the need to adapt Agile beyond the context Agile methods were initially designed for, many frameworks to scale agile have been developed in recent years. In order to understand similarities between the frameworks, we extracted a list of their underlying practices. A visualization provides a high-level overview over Scaling Agile Frameworks and enables comparison of the frameworks concerning the use of their underlying practices. Additionally, practices common to many frameworks are identified. We discuss how the results help practitioners to build their individual scaling framework. Feedback from framework authors is needed before proceeding with an in-depth analysis and comparison of the similarities and differences of the considered frameworks.

References

1. Version one: 12th annual state of agile TM report (2018). https://www.versionone.com/
2. Sutherland, J., Schwaber, K.: The scrum guide (2016). http://www.scrumguides.org
3. Scaled agile framework (2011). http://www.scaledagileframework.com/. Accessed 20 Sept 2018
4. Sutherland, J.: Scrum-of-scrums (1996). guide.agilealliance.org/guide/scrumofscrums.html
5. Laanti, M., Kettunen, P.: Finnish SAFe adoptions: a survey study. In: LargeScaleAgile@XP 2019, Montreal, Canada, 25 May 2019 (2019)
6. Putta, A., Paasivaara, M., Lassenius, C.: How are agile release trains formed in practice? A case study in a large financial corporation. In: XP 2019, 25 May 2019, Montreal, Canada (2019)
7. Quartel, R.: FAST agile scaled technology (FAST) (2015). http://www.fast-agile.com/method
8. Thompson, K.: Recipes for agile governance (RAGE) (2013). https://www.cprime.com/rage-services/
9. Kalenda, M., Hyna, P., Rossi, B.: Scaling agile in large organizations: practices, challenges, and success factors. J. Softw.: Evol. Proc. 30(10), e1954 (2018)
10. Alqudah, M., Razali, R.: A review of scaling agile methods in large software development. Int. J. Adv. Sci. Eng. Inf. Technol. 6(6), 828–837 (2016)
11. Ebert, C., Paasivaara, M.: Scaling agile. IEEE Softw. 34(6), 98–103 (2017)
12. Diebold, P., Schmitt, A., Theobald, S.: Scaling Agile – how to select the most appropriate framework. In: LargeScaleAgile@XP 2018, 21 May 2018, Porto, Portugal (2018)

13. Horlach, B., Böhmann, T., Schirmer, I., Drews, P.: IT governance in scaling agile frameworks. In: Proceedings of the Multikonferenz Wirtschaftsinformatik, Lüneburg (2018)
14. Diebold, P., Zehler, T.: The right degree of agility in rich processes. Managing Software Process Evolution, pp. 15–37. Springer, Cham (2016). https://doi.org/10.1007/978-3-319-31545-4_2
15. Agile Alliance: subway map to agile practices. https://www.agilealliance.org/agile101/subway-map-to-agile-practices/

Open Access This chapter is licensed under the terms of the Creative Commons Attribution 4.0 International License (http://creativecommons.org/licenses/by/4.0/), which permits use, sharing, adaptation, distribution and reproduction in any medium or format, as long as you give appropriate credit to the original author(s) and the source, provide a link to the Creative Commons license and indicate if changes were made.

The images or other third party material in this chapter are included in the chapter's Creative Commons license, unless indicated otherwise in a credit line to the material. If material is not included in the chapter's Creative Commons license and your intended use is not permitted by statutory regulation or exceeds the permitted use, you will need to obtain permission directly from the copyright holder.

Finnish Enterprise Agile Transformations: A Survey Study

Petri Kettunen[1]([⊠]), Maarit Laanti[2], Fabian Fagerholm[1,3],
Tommi Mikkonen[1], and Tomi Männistö[1]

[1] University of Helsinki, Helsinki, Finland
{petri.kettunen, fabian.fagerholm, tommi.mikkonen,
tomi.mannisto}@helsinki.fi
[2] Nitor Delta, Helsinki, Finland
maarit.laanti@nitor.com
[3] Blekinge University of Technology, Karlskrona, Sweden
fabian.fagerholm@bth.se

Abstract. Modern large software-intensive development organizations are nowadays more and more often believed to transform their structures and operations towards large-scale agility in search for higher performances. Based on a survey conducted in Finland in 2018, in this paper we explore the current state of the affairs with respect to how extensively organizations are actually transforming themselves, in what ways this takes place in practice and for what goals. Most of the respondents were in large organizations. The results show that the majority of the surveyed respondents indicated that their organizations have conducted agile transformations or are currently doing so. Different strategies and tactics have been used in the transformations, but markedly the respondents reported most that the company has had external consultants (subcontracting) to assist in the change. The most important goals aimed to be achieved with agile means were productivity and quality (operative) and responsiveness to customer/market changes (new features). Notably only very few respondents reported their organizations to be currently non-agile (do not use at all agile methods in software development).

Keywords: Agile transformation · Enterprise agile · Scaled agile ·
Large-scale agile software development · Survey

1 Introduction and Background

Agile methods and practices are nowadays mainstream in software development organizations. In large organizations agile software development is scaled in size to multiple teams and project program levels (large-scale agile). However, agile practices and ways of working are also increasingly applied in other functional areas and operations of large companies. Moreover, modern software-intensive companies facing digitalization are gearing to become agile enterprises – nimble and flexible with business agility [1]. These companies may be performing enterprise agile transformations.

© The Author(s) 2019
R. Hoda (Ed.): XP 2019 Workshops, LNBIP 364, pp. 97–104, 2019.
https://doi.org/10.1007/978-3-030-30126-2_12

When agile software development methods and practices are extended and scaled up to enterprise levels in large organizations, new competences and organizational capabilities beyond software engineering are required to conduct successful agile transformations [1, 2]. These include such as organization design and dynamics, production economics and product/service solution management which are all distinct disciplines of their own. Each organization should know their needs and goals of agility [3, 4].

Agile research tends to be lagging behind industrial practice. Assuming that large companies are in reality performing agile transformations, there is a need for more empirical research. Relevant research topics include how to conduct large-scale agile transformations, what the important context factors are, and what the role of the established agile scaling frameworks (e.g., SAFe) is [5]. Our research problem is to understand why and how different companies want to change with agile means including whether companies have conducted agile transformations and to what extent, and how beneficial and successful their particular changes have been. Digitalization is one of our key context factors. In this paper we present current results with respect to agile transformations in large organizations based on our recent survey study done in Finland. We have reported related results about agile scaling frameworks (SAFe) elsewhere [6]. Notably here we see scaled agile in software development as a means for enterprise-level agility in larger organizations.

Various Agile surveys have been conducted earlier, but nowadays especially the fast progress of digitalization makes it topical for different organizations. Agile is expanding from pure software industry to traditional, non-software industries and scaling in enterprises. Considering prior and related survey works, one of the most internationally known ones is the annual State of Agile survey by Version One [7]. In Finland a particular scientific survey was done in 2012 [8]. In addition, the annual Finnish Software Industry Survey has addressed agility-related points [9]. Our guiding motivations for this survey research were to investigate the current state of the agile development in Finland taking into account enterprise-level agility and also non-ICT companies.

2   Survey Research Design

The overall purpose of our survey research was to examine the current state of Agile and enterprise agility in Finland. To begin with, we were interested in measuring how widely agile methods and practices are currently applied in industrial practice and how that is evolving.

Following this line of thinking we defined a broad range of topics and issues ranging from basic ones of agile software methods and practices to company-wide matters. Moreover, we aimed to investigate not only the current whereabouts but also the future intentions of the companies. The target population was intentionally not limited to software companies since we were also interested in non-software companies currently facing digitalization and becoming more software-intensive (i.e., companies in other industries than IT).

The survey questionnaire was composed by starting from our selected main research themes and interests stated above. The questionnaire structure comprised the following primary sections:

1. Company's state of agile
2. Agile company transformation
3. Agile future of the company

The specific questions were compiled on the one hand by referring to prior surveys for comparison purposes (e.g., [7, 8]) and by deriving from our industrial experiences and our prior works (e.g., [3]) on the other hand. The draft questionnaire was first piloted both in our industrial and academic organizations. The final version consisted of total of 50 questions (including background information items). Certain questions were only applicable depending on their preceding selector questions (e.g., whether SAFe is in use or not). The survey was available in both Finnish and in English (translated by the first author).

For data collection the survey was implemented as a web-based online questionnaire with the Finnish/English language choice. The questionnaire was distributed through social media and a proprietary industrial mailing list mass postings to over 600 people, and it was open for responding for four weeks during November and December 2018.

3   Results

In this paper we present the subset of the full survey result data directly related to the research topic of large agile transformations. In the survey the following questions addressed specifically that area:

- *When has there been executed or planned agile transformation in Your company most recently?*[1]
  - The question was instructed as follows: "Extensive (covering the entire software development) change to adopt agile methods, practices and ways of working"
- *How is Your company/has Your company been executing agile transformation?*
- *Why does Your company want to become more agile?*
- *Is Your company conducting or planning an agile transformation?*
  - This question was applicable for non-agile company respondents only (i.e., the ones who reported their company not to use agile methods at all).

Next, we present the results data of the above main questions. A total of over 400 replies were received, but only 28% of the respondents finished the questionnaire. Not all replied to all questions. In this paper, we report only on the data of those respondents (119) who replied to the last question in the questionnaire sequence (background

---

[1] In this paper we show the English translations of the Finnish questions regardless of which language the respondents have used.

information of the respondent). In our web-tool implementation of the questionnaire we did not restrict the finishing with mandatory questions.

The key respondent demographic information is presented in Tables 1 and 2. Notably most of the respondents (74%) were from large or very large organizations.

Table 1. What is the size of Your organization?

(multi choice not allowed)	n (N = 119, 'No answer' choice N/A = 4)	% (out of N)
Very large (more than 5000 persons)	45	38
Large (more than 250 persons)	43	36
Middle-sized (50–250 persons	12	10
Small (10–50 persons)	12	10
Micro (less than 10 persons)	3	3

Table 2. What is the primary sector (line of business) of Your company?

(top 3) (multi choice not allowed)	n (N = 117, N/A = 2)	%
C1 ICT sector (including consulting), information technology	39	33
C2 Financial sector (banking, insurance)	27	23
C4 Telecom services	13	11

Table 3 shows that approximately 40% of the responses indicated that the respondents' organizations have already conducted agile transformations ('Done') while 30% stated that they are currently (at the time of the survey in 2018) doing that ('In progress'). Furthermore, it tabulates the distributions according to the top industry sectors (see Table 2).

Table 3. When has there been executed or planned agile transformation in Your company most recently?

(multi choice allowed)	n (N = 117, N/A = 6)	% (out of N)	C1 (N = 34)	C2 (N = 27)	C4 (N = 13)
Done over 5 years ago	15	13	11	0	1
Done 2–5 years ago	22	19	9	3	6
Done some one year ago	14	12	1	3	2
In progress	35	30	5	16	5
Planned, implementation schedule open	8	7	2	3	0
Under planning (e.g., pilots)	5	4	0	4	0
Not done/planned agile transformation	20	17	8	1	0

Table 4 gives insights about how the respondents perceived their organizations' transformations conducted in practice. The organizations have applied both bottom-up and top-down approaches to their transformations. The respondents indicated the utilization of external consulting support most (43%).

Table 4. How is Your company/has Your company been executing agile transformation?

(multi choice allowed)	n (N = 84, N/A = 2)	% (out of N)
The company has a strategy for adopting agile ways of working and practices	24	29
The company has initiated the change top-down in the organization	26	31
The company has initiated the change bottom-up (from teams) in the organization	34	40
There is a dedicated agile support team in the company	37	44
The company has had external consultants (subcontracting) to assist in the change	51	61
Self-made transformation in the company	13	15
In other ways (how)	5	6

We did not ask directly why companies conduct their agile transformations. However, insights to that can be inferred from what goals they target to achieve with agility. Table 5 summarizes what the respondents ranked the five most important reasons for becoming agile for their organizations.

Table 5. Why does Your company want to become more agile?

(top 5, multi choice allowed)	n (N = 85, N/A = 2)	% (out of N)
Productivity and quality (operative)	62	73
Responsiveness to customer/market changes (new features)	56	66
Job satisfaction	46	54
Fast/continuous organizational learning in rapidly changing operating environments	43	51
Competitive and desirable products (new product development)	41	48

Finally, in contrast we were also interested in non-agile organizations (i.e., who respond to the question: 'How widely does Your company use agile methods in software development? – We do not use at all'). Only 6 out of the 119 respondents were in non-agile organizations. Most of them (5) stated that their organization are not active to transform, either ('Is Your company conducting or planning an agile transformation? – Not in progress/planning').

4 Discussion

Our key discovery in this study is that agile transformations have been conducted in this Finnish sample of organizations already several years ago (see Table 3). They are also ongoing in different industry sectors.

Another key insight is that different large organizations appear to be using different strategies and tactics for their agile transformations (see Table 4). There is emphasis to have external consultants (subcontracting) to assist in the change. That could indicate that the companies have realized to need new competencies and/or additional resources to perform their transformations in sustainable ways. Unsurprisingly company internal efficiencies were scored the highest goals to be attained with agile means but also the external, customer-related goals of agility are important. Such performance effects require systematic company-wide capabilities that agile transformations may bring.

In comparison to the related studies, Rodríguez et al. investigated agile and lean adoption (usage of agile and lean methods) in software developing organizations [8]. They do not address agile transformation in the large organizational scale like we do. With respect to our results ('The company has initiated the change top-down in the organization' in Table 4) one particular comparable point in their study was that top management commitment was the most significant challenge in agile and lean adoption. Like in our results (Table 5), productivity was the most important goal. Notably, though, in our survey questionnaire agile and lean were not combined.

VersionOne also reports agile adoption (usage of agile practices) rather than *transformation* [7]. However, their 2018 survey concludes that "agile is expanding within the enterprise" for instance with product roadmapping. One comparable result point in their study is that 30% of the respondents' organizations have been practicing agile development methods for more than 5 years while in our case some 13% of the respondents reported their organizations to have performed agile transformation in that time frame ('Done over 5 years ago' in Table 3). In contrast to our results (Table 5) and the study by Rodríguez et al. [8], the most important goal for agile adoption was reported to be accelerated delivery speed while productivity was ranked third.

With respect to non-agile organizations VersionOne reports that 97% of respondents' organizations practice agile development methods [7]. In our survey the comparative value is 94%. Strikingly, Rodríguez et al. reported 42% of organizational units with no agile nor lean methods usage [8]. This could be due to the differences in the sample population or that the organizations have progressed since that time (2012).

Considering the comparability and generalization, we acknowledge that a validity concern in our results is whether all the respondents have interpreted and conceived the term *agile transformation* in the same way ('Extensive (covering the entire software development) change to adopt agile methods, practices and ways of working'). However, also Rodríguez et al. did not limit the usage of agile with specific definitions [8].

A general limitation due to our survey design is that we did not ask the respondents to identify their organization. Consequently, we cannot tell the number of different responding companies. Rodríguez et al. acknowledged the same in this kind of survey research [8]. Due to the confidentiality reasons we refrain from evaluating how representative our respondent sample is with respect to all Finnish industries. However, the respondents represented several different business domains (see Table 2).

5   Conclusions

Based on a recent survey conducted in Finland in 2018, in this paper we have explored the current state of Agile with respect to how extensively organizations are actually transforming themselves and in what ways in practice. Most of the surveyed respondents perceived to be in organizations which have already conducted agile transformations or are currently doing so. Different organizations have used different strategies and tactics but external consultant support is often utilized.

Further work will be done to analyze the survey results more broadly and deeply with cross-tabulations covering more questions than was possible in here. Digitalization may affect companies in different business domains and industries differently.

Our future research plans include repeating the survey study in certain other countries and also annually in Finland. That would make it possible to do more extensive comparative and longitudinal analysis.

Furthermore, our questionnaire can be refined and improved based on the experiences of this first survey round. Considering large agile transformations, a refinement could be to enquire whether the transformation covers the company fully (enterprise agility) or partially – and how exactly (only software development/IT or certain functions/levels) [10, 11]. Additional context factors to support the results analysis could be what particular business environment variables, regulations, certifications or other such requirements and constraints influence the software development of the company. Naturally, already the business domains (Table 2) inform such factors in general.

References

1. Kettunen, P., Laanti, M.: Future software organizations – agile goals and roles. Eur. J. Futures Res. **5**, 16 (2017)
2. Kettunen, P., Laanti, M.: Combining agile software projects and large-scale organizational agility. Softw. Process: Improv. Pract. **13**(2), 183–193 (2008)
3. Kettunen, P.: Systematizing software-development agility: toward an enterprise capability improvement framework. J. Enterp. Transform. **2**(2), 81–104 (2012)
4. Laanti, M.: Agile transformation model for large software development organizations. In: Proceedings of the XP2017 Scientific Workshops, Article No. 19. ACM, New York (2017)
5. Moe, N.B., Dingsøyr, T.: Emerging research themes and updated research agenda for large-scale agile development: a summary of the 5th international workshop at XP2017. In: Proceedings of the XP2017 Scientific Workshops, Article No. 14. ACM, New York, (2017)
6. Laanti, M., Kettunen, P.: SAFe adoptions in Finland: a survey research. In: XP 2019 7th International Workshop on Large-Scale Agile Development (LargeScaleAgile) (in press)
7. Version One 12th Annual State of Agile Report. https://stateofagile.versionone.com. (conducted between August and December 2017). Accessed 10 Mar 2019

8. Rodríguez, P., Markkula, J., Oivo, M., Turula, K.: Survey on agile and lean usage in finnish software industry. In: ESEM 2012 Proceedings of the ACM-IEEE International Symposium on Empirical Software Engineering and Measurement, pp. 139–148. ACM, New York (2012)
9. Finnish Software Industry Survey. http://www.softwareindustrysurvey.fi/focus-on-flexibility-agility-in-software-development/. Accessed 10 Mar 2019
10. Goldman, S.L., Nagel, R.N., Preiss, K.: Agile Competitors and Virtual Organizations: Strategies for Enriching the Customer. Van Nostrand Reinhold, New York (1995)
11. Ronzon, T., Buck, J., Eckstein, J.: Making companies nimble – from software agility to business agility. IEEE Softw. **36**(1), 79–85 (2019)

Open Access This chapter is licensed under the terms of the Creative Commons Attribution 4.0 International License (http://creativecommons.org/licenses/by/4.0/), which permits use, sharing, adaptation, distribution and reproduction in any medium or format, as long as you give appropriate credit to the original author(s) and the source, provide a link to the Creative Commons license and indicate if changes were made.

The images or other third party material in this chapter are included in the chapter's Creative Commons license, unless indicated otherwise in a credit line to the material. If material is not included in the chapter's Creative Commons license and your intended use is not permitted by statutory regulation or exceeds the permitted use, you will need to obtain permission directly from the copyright holder.

Changes Over Time in a Planned Inter-team Coordination Routine

Tomas Gustavsson[(✉)] [iD]

Karlstad University, Karlstad, Sweden
tomas.gustavsson@kau.se

Abstract. The benefits of agile ways of working in small teams have inspired larger organizations to implement large-scale agile frameworks. To manage dependencies between teams, there is a need for routines to plan and divide work between teams as well as routines to manage emerging dependency issues. These routines are often changed over time, but how tailoring is performed is not much studied. This study aims to fill that gap by presenting the tailoring of a planned coordination routine in three organizations over a period of one and a half year. By visiting planning sessions, 379 h of observation data were collected. Investigating details of this routine gives a much more dynamic view, compared to the static description presented in the framework. Different logics for tailoring could be seen in the three cases. For deciding on a cadence for the planning period, three diverse logics were used as the basis for the decisions: knowledge, time, and resources.

Keywords: Inter-team coordination · Large-scale ·
Agile software development · Scaled agile framework · Routine dynamics

1 Introduction

There is an industry trend towards adopting agile methodologies in-the-large, and although research into agile software development (ASD) has matured in the past years, agile in large-scale settings are not much explored [1]. Although some studies are reported from large-scale transformations, such as the presented studies in Dikert, Paasivaara, and Lassenius [2], there are few studies investigating implementations of large-scale agile frameworks. This study can help to bridge that gap.

A suggested future research agenda for large-scale ASD was a call for further research in how coordination change over time [3]. Coordination can either be planned, such as dividing work in advance and identifying dependencies or designed to deal with emerging dependency issues, such as daily or weekly meetings to solve problems [4]. Different ways to coordinate are sometimes called practices [5], mechanisms [5, 7], or routines [4]. Feldman and Pentland define organizational routines (hereafter, simply *routines*) as "repetitive, recognizable patterns of interdependent actions, carried out by multiple actors" [7, p. 94] which well describes different ways of coordination and therefore the term routine will be used henceforth.

For example, Dietrich et al. [5] studied the different types of coordination routines on individual versus group mode used in large-scale ASD, and Dingsøyr et al. [6]

© The Author(s) 2019
R. Hoda (Ed.): XP 2019 Workshops, LNBIP 364, pp. 105–111, 2019.
https://doi.org/10.1007/978-3-030-30126-2_13

studied different types of coordination routines used in a large-scale ASD program and how they evolved. Both studies present a list of routines for coordination in large-scale agile settings but do not investigate in detail how the routines were changed or tailored in detail from a performative aspect. This paper focuses on the details of one specific planned coordination routine performed in large-scale ASD with the research question: *How is the PI planning routine tailored in SAFe implementations?*

To answer the research questions, three case organizations were investigated: Auto, a product development department within the Automotive industry. Gov, a project at a Government Agency in Sweden, and Bank, a development department in one of the four largest business banks in Sweden. The observations at these case organizations started when they implemented the Scaled Agile Framework (SAFe), and observations went on for one and a half year.

2   The PI Planning Coordination Routines in SAFe

SAFe consists of a number of roles, artifacts, and routines, and this is a brief description of one investigated routine for planned inter-team coordination. PI planning, as described in SAFe [7], is a routine for dividing work and identifying dependencies between teams for a set period of time into the future. SAFe explains that "PIs are typically 8–12 weeks long. The most common pattern for a PI is four development Iterations, followed by one Innovation and Planning (IP) Iteration" [7]. According to SAFe, the typical iteration is hence two weeks long.

The importance of PI planning is explained on the website: "PI planning is essential to SAFe: If you are not doing it, you are not doing SAFe" [7]. The routine follows a strict two-day agenda (see Fig. 1) where the first half day comprises different presentations followed by "Team Breakouts" where each team plans their work.

The first day ends with a presentation and review of a draft plan and the first half of the second day is used for adjustments and further planning and ends with a presentation and review of the final plan. The second, and last, part of the second day comprises risk management, a confidence vote (in which teams vote on their confidence in meeting their planned PI objectives) and a joint retrospective for all teams and stakeholders participating in the PI planning workshop. Depending on the result of the final plan review and confidence vote, an undefined amount of time [8] is set aside for rework of the plan to be finalized before the end of the second day. Out of the two full days, only five hours (30%) is dedicated for team breakout time.

Something that is not visualized in the standard agenda is to conduct a number of inter-team meetings called Scrum of Scrums (SoS) during the team breakout sessions where all Scrum Masters attend to follow up if teams are following the intended planning schedule. A number of questions are raised in these meetings such as "Has capacity (velocity) been identified for each iteration?", "Have any program risks been identified?", and "Have dependencies with other teams been identified and/or resolved?" [9]. These meetings are also called *SoS Sync* to differ them from the ordinary SoS meetings which are conducted during the program increment, often two or three times a week, to sort out emerging team dependency issues [8].

Fig. 1. PI planning standard agenda. (source: Scaled Agile Framework [8]).

As can be seen, the way to conduct PI planning is expressed in a prescribed manner regarding the steps to be performed. Conboy and Carroll [10] put forth, in a study of 13 agile transformations, that the risk of implementing a common framework is that it imposes too many restrictions and rigidity on the employees. On the other hand, the lack of guidelines from a common framework may lead to a lack of common direction in the agile implementation as Paasivaara et al. [11] pointed out from studying the company Ericsson.

3   Method

Observations, using field notes and photographs, together with memoranda from meetings, were used as data for the study. On-site visits and observations in the various cases are presented in Table 1. Results are presented in a tabular format as well as a short narrative describing the identified results. The analysis is comprised of investigating and comparing differences between the detailed prescribed way of conducting PI planning according to SAFe and how the PI planning routine was performed in the three cases. The studied organizations (Auto, Gov, and Bank), had a history of agile ways of working between four to six years before starting to implement SAFe. The cases were chosen because they all had experience and maturity in agile ways of working, since the study focuses on the implementation of a large-scale framework, not implementing ASD per se. Also, it was essential to select cases which were at the beginning of implementing the SAFe framework, to be able to follow tailoring from the very starting point. The teams at Bank and Gov were each organized as one unit, also called an Agile Release Train (ART) [8]. At Auto, they were divided into three ARTs, hence the many hours spent on observation in this organization compared to the other two cases.

Table 1. The number of on-site visits and hours of observation.

Case	# of on-site visits	Hours of observation
Auto	6	196
Gov	5	113
Bank	6	70
Total	**17**	**379**

The on-site observations were conducted during a number of PI planning workshops, from April 2017 until November 2018, a period of one and a half years, as depicted in Fig. 2.

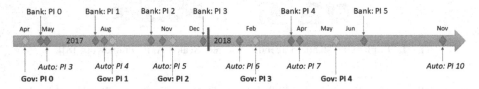

Fig. 2. On-site observations at the case organizations.

Data was collected from the starting point of the implementation of SAFe at Bank and Gov while Auto had started their transformation three months prior to the first observation and had already conducted two PI planning workshops.

4   Results

The results presented in Table 2 are from the first and the last observed PI planning workshop.

Table 2. Data from PI planning at Auto, Gov, and Bank from the first and last observation.

Case	Auto PI 3	Gov PI 1	Bank PI 0	Auto PI 10	Gov PI 4	Bank PI 5
Number of weeks per PI	10	12	6	10	15	11
Number of iterations per PI	3	4	2	3	5	4
Iteration length (weeks)	3	3	2,5	3	3	2,5
Length of final IP iteration	1 week	2,5 days	None	1 week	2,5 days	2,5 days
PI planning workshop (hours)	12	15	10	11,5	12	12
Number of SoS syncs	3	2	2	2	0	5
Number of SoS sync questions	8	7	13	8	0	5
Team breakout time (hours)	5,5	4,5	4,9	7,5	8	7,5
Team breakout time (percent)	45,8%	30%	49%	65,2%	66,7%	62,5%

Auto was conducting their third PI planning during the first observation, and all three ARTs had decided on a set 10-week cadence, all three within the same week. The cadence remained the same all through the observation period but the agenda changed over time, mainly by removing common presentations and adding time for team breakout sessions. Amount of time for team breakout changed from 45,8% of time used for PI planning up till 65,2% in the last observed session.

PI 0 at Gov was not a real PI planning but a one-day information workshop to incur buy-in of SAFe to the five teams and let them meet physically since two teams had their home office in another city. A follow-up from the first real PI planning, PI 1, showed lots of negative feedback where draft plan reviews and risk resolving meetings were mainly seen as waste and "unhelpful status meetings". Gov did not use time as a basis for cadence but instead the amount of resources, in this case, available man-hours. For the summer months, PI:s were longer since many employees go on vacation.

Negative comments were also put forth regarding the SoS sync meetings at Gov. Gov started out with two SoS sync meetings during their first PI planning, where scrum masters answered seven questions twice during the two-day workshop. In their second PI planning, they only held one SoS sync meeting, and in the third PI planning, they abandoned the SoS sync entirely. Auto started out with three SoS syncs but later reduced this to two SoS syncs per PI planning, still keeping the same format with eight follow-up questions. Bank, on the other hand, started with two longer SoS syncs, answering as much as thirteen follow-up questions but changed the format to become shorter (only five questions to answer) and more often (five times per PI planning).

At Bank, the first PI was only aimed at planning two sprints and not, as prescribed by SAFe, intended to become a set cadence. Instead, Bank proposed shorter PIs during the first PI planning sessions in order to train team members and to get shorter feedback loops on tailoring the PI planning routine. During the last observation, PI 5, four sprints had been used as PI length for two times, and Bank did not see any benefits in reaching for more extended planning periods. Instead, four sprints became the fixed cadence for future PI planning workshops.

5 Discussion

The planned coordination routine called PI planning is described in SAFe as a two-day workshop with a prescribed standardized two-day agenda where teams in an ART plan according to a fixed cadence "typically 8–12 weeks long" where the "most common pattern for a PI is four development Iterations, followed by one Innovation and Planning (IP) Iteration" [8]. But is this a proper PI format and is the proposed standard schedule a suitable format for PI planning? Since the second most reported obstacle reported in Laanti and Kettunen [12] was that SAFe was not fitted correctly to the organization, tailoring is probably needed. But how could the planning routine be tailored? Three organizations with disparate business logics were investigated to answer the research question: *How is the PI planning routine tailored in SAFe implementations?*

Investigating details of this specific planned coordination routine in the three case organizations gives a much more dynamic view, compared to the static description presented in SAFe [8]. The planning periods observed ranged from 6 to 15 weeks and at Bank, deciding on a set cadence from the start was not the intention. Instead, the logic at Bank was during the beginning of implementation to have shorter feedback loops to be able to tailor PI planning according to the needs of the ART. At Gov, the cadence was based on amount of resources available, meaning that PI:s during spring or fall were shorter than in the summertime since more employees go on vacation in the summertime. Deciding on a cadence for a PI can, as can be seen in the three cases, be based on different logics. In the Bank case, the length of the planning period was decided based on having short early feedback loops to learn how to conduct PI planning quickly. At Gov, the same amount of available resources was the basis for the length of the PI while Auto used what SAFe prescribes: the same number of weeks per PI. Also, although SAFe claim two weeks to be the typical length of iterations, this was not true in any of the cases as they all preferred longer iteration times: 2,5 versus 3 weeks in length.

In all three organizations, feedback from the teams was that too much time was spent in joint meetings which were mainly seen as waste. Time was instead added for teams to plan, the so-called Team Breakout sessions. At Gov, the first PI planning workshop was conducted according to SAFe prescription with 30% of the time spent in Team Breakout, the least amount of Team Breakout time compared to Auto and Bank. At the last observed PI planning workshop at Gov, teams spent 66,7% of their time in Team Breakouts. The increased amount of time spent in Team Breakout was also seen at Auto and Bank. This suggests that organizations implementing SAFe values Team Breakout more than other suggested items in the PI planning schedule.

Although the time-span of the PI during the last PI planning was within suggestions from SAFe (8–12 weeks) at two of the organizations and one even longer (15 weeks at Gov), none of the organizations felt the need for more than one and a half day to plan. This suggests that the suggested amount of time to plan is perceived as unnecessary long.

Planned PIs consisted of three to five sprints, and Auto was the only case which had an actual IP iteration at the end of the PI (which lasted for one week). Both Gov and Bank only allowed one day for innovation and the rest of the time (1,5 days) for planning the next PI. This is somewhat surprising since a basic idea of SAFe is to have time set aside for improvement and innovation [8]. An area for future research is to investigate why such little time is allowed for improvement and innovation in some organizations and the implications of these different approaches. Are organizations who allow more time for innovation more innovative or does not the allowed time for improvement have the intended effects?

References

1. Moe, N.B., Olsson, H.H., Dingsøyr, T.: Trends in large-scale agile development: a summary of the 4th workshop at XP2016. In: Proceedings of the XP2016 Scientific Workshop (2016)
2. Dikert, K., Paasivaara, M., Lassenius, C.: Challenges and success factors for large-scale agile transformations: a systematic literature review. J. Syst. Softw. **119**, 87–108 (2016)

3. Moe, N.B., Dingsøyr, T.: Emerging research themes and updated research agenda for large-scale agile development: a summary of the 5th international workshop at XP2017. In: Proceedings of the XP2017 Scientific Workshops (2017)
4. Okhuysen, G.A., Bechky, B.A.: Coordination in organizations: an integrative perspective. Acad. Manag. Ann. **3**(1), 463–502 (2009)
5. Dietrich, P., Kujala, J., Artto, K.: Inter-team coordination patterns and outcomes in multi-team projects. Proj. Manag. J. **44**(6), 6–19 (2013)
6. Dingsøyr, T., Moe, N.B., Seim, E.A.: Coordinating knowledge work in multi-team programs: findings from a large-scale agile development program. Proj. Manag. J. **49**(6), 64–77 (2018)
7. Feldman, M.S., Pentland, B.T.: Reconceptualizing organizational routines as a source of flexibility and change. Adm. Sci. Q. **48**, 94–118 (2003)
8. Scaled Agile Framework 4.6. www.scaledagileframework.org. Accessed 22 Feb 2019
9. Tech Academy PI Planning. safe.tech-academy.co.uk/pi-planning/. Accessed 3 Mar 2019
10. Conboy, K., Carroll, N.: Implementing large-scale agile frameworks: challenges and recommendations. IEEE Softw. **36**, 44–50 (2019)
11. Paasivaara, M., Behm, B., Lassenius, C., Hallikainen, M.: Large-scale agile transformation at Ericsson: a case study. Empir. Softw. Eng. **23**(5), 2550–2596 (2018)
12. Laanti, M., Kettunen, P.: Finnish SAFe adoptions: a survey study. In: Proceedings of the XP2019 Scientific Workshops, Montreal, Canada, 21–25 May 2019

Open Access This chapter is licensed under the terms of the Creative Commons Attribution 4.0 International License (http://creativecommons.org/licenses/by/4.0/), which permits use, sharing, adaptation, distribution and reproduction in any medium or format, as long as you give appropriate credit to the original author(s) and the source, provide a link to the Creative Commons license and indicate if changes were made.

The images or other third party material in this chapter are included in the chapter's Creative Commons license, unless indicated otherwise in a credit line to the material. If material is not included in the chapter's Creative Commons license and your intended use is not permitted by statutory regulation or exceeds the permitted use, you will need to obtain permission directly from the copyright holder.

Technical-, Social- and Process Debt in Large-Scale Agile: An Exploratory Case-Study

Antonio Martini[1]([✉]), Viktoria Stray[1,2]([✉]), and Nils Brede Moe[2]([✉])

[1] Department of Informatics, University of Oslo, Oslo, Norway
{antonima, stray}@ifi.uio.no
[2] SINTEF, Trondheim, Norway
nils.b.moe@sintef.no

Abstract. Large-scale agile projects bring inter-teams interaction challenges. Teams need to be autonomous, but often crosscutting concerns affect many teams. If the teams fail to collaborate on these concerns, the negative effects might hinder agility in the medium and long term. In other words, the organization and the system accumulate *debt*, on which the teams pay a high interest. Such debt must therefore be prioritized and "repaid" timely. We conducted a case study with interviews, observations and document analysis. Via both team- and large-scale retrospectives we investigated how teams coordinate and discuss Technical-, Social- and Process Debts.

Keywords: Large-scale software development · Coordination practices · Communication · Technical debt · Process debt · Social debt · Retrospective

1 Introduction

Large software companies strive to become more responsive in identifying and satisfying their customers' needs. One strategy for increasing responsiveness is the introduction of autonomous teams and agile software development [14]. However, when many agile teams are working towards the same goal in a Large-Scale Agile (LSA) project, a lot of coordination and management effort is required [13]. If each of the autonomous team in LSA setting works independently, team development processes and technical solutions would ultimately differ and may be highly disconnected from one another. Further, a high level of team autonomy and a need for constant delivering value to the customer, can lead to sub-optimal processes that might have short-term benefits, but generates a negative impact for the organization in the medium-long term. Examples of negative impact can be duplicated work, misunderstandings and integration problems.

In recent literature, a financial metaphor has been successfully used to describe such phenomena: aiming for short-term goals is equivalent to taking a *debt*, and the additional negative impact paid in the medium-long term is considered the *interest* that is paid on such debt. Although the metaphor has been used to describe prevalently technical issues (hence the term Technical Debt [4]), the debt metaphor has been used

© The Author(s) 2019
R. Hoda (Ed.): XP 2019 Workshops, LNBIP 364, pp. 112–119, 2019.
https://doi.org/10.1007/978-3-030-30126-2_14

to describe other kinds of sub-optimal solutions, for example related to the social structure of the development community (Social Debt [16]) or to the development processes (Process Debt [1, 8]). However, how different types of Debt are identified and managed in LSA, is still an open question.

As an example, let us take what is called *Architectural Debt*: in LSA, system cross-cutting concerns (e.g. maintainability, usability and performance) and the consequent technical solutions, need to be envisioned at a higher level than from a single team perspective. As an example, if the concerns are not well separated in the system (which represents the Architectural Debt), several teams might find themselves working on the same shared component. Changing the same component in parallel, hinders the teams; they have to coordinate, merge conflicts and share the responsibility of the component. This, in the end, either creates a lot of overhead for the teams or causes the component quality to degrade, making future changes problematic (these effects are the interest paid on the debt). Communication is key to avoid these problems and might not happen if not supported by practices shared across the teams.

Recent literature in LSA has provided a better understanding on how teams coordinate; Dingsøyr et al. [5] describe 14 mechanisms for inter-team coordination in large-scale software projects. They found that coordination of work between teams influences teams' internal processes and how each team makes decisions. Nyrud and Stray [11] identified 11 coordination mechanisms in a large-scale agile project and found retrospective meetings to be important for continuous improvement of the inter-team coordination mechanisms. Further, managers need to be sensitive to the coordination needs as they change over time in large programs [10].

However, to the best of our knowledge, there are no related studies addressing the challenge of balancing the management of technical-, social- and Process Debt in LSA. We aimed to understand which types of debt that require inter-team coordination in LSA by answering the following research question:

RQ: What types of debt are elicited and discussed on team level and inter-team level in a large-scale agile project?

2   Technical-, Social- and Process Debt

Different types of debts have been researched. However, Technical Debt (TD) is the one for which the most literature is available. The definition of TD is [2]:

> " [...]a collection of design or implementation constructs that are expedient in the short term, but set up a technical context that can make future changes more costly or impossible. [...]".

Different types of TD have been identified. The most common ones are [8]:

- **Code Debt,** which is related to sub-optimal code solutions. For example, not declaring a variable that later requires manually changing all the instances in the code.
- **Architectural Debt** is regarded as sub-optimal solutions with respect to an ideal architecture. For example, a monolithic architecture with many dependencies across

modules requires teams to change the code in many places for any change. This might require more time to deliver features and might introduce bugs.

- **Test Debt** is regarded as lack or sub-optimal tests. For example, low code coverage or the lack of structured and automated tests can be considered test debts.
- **Documentation Debt** is the lack or sub-optimal documentation. An example could be the lack of description on how APIs work, which hinders developers when correctly accessing modules, components or services across the system.
- **Infrastructure Debt** is related to sub-optimal solutions in the development environment. For example, buggy knowledge management tools.

Other types of debt (non-technical) have also been identified in literature as causing negative impact, namely Social Debt and Process Debt.

As for **Social Debt**, it is referred to as *"the presence of sub-optimality in the development community, which causes a negative effect"* [16]. An example of Social Debt is the lack of proper communication among key parts of the organizations (e.g. between development and operations). Another example is having an architecture team that is disconnected from the team and therefore might suggest architectural solutions that are not realistic, as they do not take into consideration details and requirements elicited during implementation.

On the other hand, **Process Debt** is mentioned as a type of debt that needs to be managed [1, 8], but there exists no current definition for it. We therefore use our own operational definition based on the ones reported for the other types of debt. We define Process Debt as *"a sub-optimal activity or process that might have short-term benefits, but generates a negative impact in the medium-long term"*. An example of Process Debt might be that teams conduct stand-up meetings where the focus is reporting status so that the leader knows what is going on [15]. The short-term benefit is that the team members satisfy their leader's need for knowing project status. However, a long-term negative impact is that the meeting centers around reporting and not about sharing knowledge and solving dependencies which is more valuable in the medium-long term. Another example is a large-scale project having the presence of many meetings to coordinate, which might seem important for solving dependencies, but disrupts the development work compromising the project efficiency [3, 15].

3   Research Methodology

Since the goal of this research was to explore and provide insight into the phenomenon of both technical and non-Technical Debt in LSA, we designed a case study [18] to observe the various types of debt in practice. We chose a large-scale project that develops a new platform supporting public transportation as our case. The project has thirteen development teams ranging between five and fourteen team members working towards the same products.

Understanding the design or implementation constructs that are expedient in the short term, but that can make future changes more costly or impossible is a complex problem. There is a need to understand challenges and improvement suggestions together with what is working well. Further, there is a need to get many stakeholders of the LSA project together as no one in an LSA project has the full overview of the situation. Also, the teams need to discuss issues that (potentially) negatively impact one or more teams and involve more than one team (inter-teams) such as shared components.

Conducting retrospective meetings is an important and popular practice in agile software development [17], and applied both on team-level and in large-scale agile [6]. The meetings are utilized for improving the way of working, and participants often discuss past challenges and how to overcome them to work better together in the future [7]. Therefore, we chose retrospectives as the primary source of our data collection for studying our research question. We chose to study team-level retrospectives (see Fig. 1) and a large-scale retrospective. Additionally, we conducted two informal group interviews to prepare for the retrospective sessions. All the six reports from the meetings were imported into NVivo. We analyzed the meetings by categorizing the reported issues into the different type of debts described in the background section.

Fig. 1. Issues discussed during one of the team retrospectives using DAKI

- **Team Retrospectives**: In November 2017 we facilitated a retrospective meeting in Team Alpha (see Fig. 1). This retrospective meeting had eight team members present. We also collected four reports from their previous retrospective meetings. These reports included what had been reported as positive and negative issues in addition to action items (often with a person responsible for following up the item). These retrospectives had been held between December 2016 and September 2017.
- **Large-Scale Retrospective**: We facilitated a retrospective meeting with project leaders, product owners and the team leaders in the LSA project; 13 people in total. The focus in this retrospective was on a large delivery they had been working on from May to November 2nd, 2017. To elicit the relevant problems we chose to use an exercise where participants discuss issues that need to be dropped, added, kept or improved (DAKI) [12]. This exercise uses four quadrants where participants can

place issues and is good to use when there is a high number of participants and issues. We then facilitated a discussion of the most urgent items by using the technique Lean Coffee [9] (Table 1).

Table 1. Data collection

Data	Explanation	Number
Informal group interviews	Questions about the teams, how they were working, the roles and their retrospective meetings	2
Retrospective reports Retrospective meeting in one team Large-scale retrospective	We collected reports from Team Alpha We facilitated a retrospective in Team Alpha We facilitated a retrospective meeting with representatives from teams in the LSA project	4 1 1

4 Results

We observed which different types of debt were discussed in team retrospectives compared to a large-scale retrospective. This would tell us if some types of debts seem to be more team issues (and would not require coordination) rather than inter-team issues.

We therefore report such comparison by counting the number of issues for each type of debt in Table 2. First, we outline the difference between Process, Social Debt and overall Technical Debt. Then, we show the number of issues related to the sub-types of Technical Debt. We omit Code Debt, as we did not find any Code Debt issue discussed.

Table 2. Number of issues discussed in team and large-scale retrospectives

Debt type	Team retrospectives	Large-scale retrospectives
Process debt	24	17
Social debt	37	15
Technical debt	26	11
Architecture debt	6	2
Documentation debt	7	2
Infrastructure debt	7	2
Test debt	6	5

We report, in Table 3, the issues that were discussed in both team retrospectives and LS retrospectives, as well as some of the issues that were instead discussed only on a team level. This would show the difference between which issues were autonomously addressed and which ones required coordination. Below the table, we list the only two issues that were brought up during the large-scale session only (related to Test Debt).

Table 3. Issues that were discussed by teams only and issues that were re-proposed for inter-team discussion and coordination

Debt type	Re-proposed at inter-team level	Team retrospectives only
Architecture debt	• Unstable APIs (teams modifying often) • Unclear module responsibilities (more structure needed)	• Deployment issues
Documentation debt	• Need for spread the documentation across teams	• Documentation issues for specific modules
Infrastructure debt	• Problems related to Jira and its usage for stories and epics	• Issues related to a specific knowledge management tool used by the team
Test debt*	• More automated tests • More test follow-up	• Test coverage • Specific test structure
Process debt	• Have more demo sessions • More and better structured planning • More meetings preparation and effectiveness (too many people) • Specific release event not well executed • More pair-programming • Agile definition (e.g. sprint definition)	• Issues related to a specific team process (e.g. team planning)
Social debt	• Team autonomy • Involvement and synchronization with leadership • Sync with POs, PMs, etc • Information and knowledge across teams • Common goals • Communication and involvement of UX developers	• Slack usage and content • Team specific roles (e.g. specific module testing responsibility) • Team specific competences (e.g. UX, design)

*Test Debt issues that were discussed on Large-Scale Retrospectives only:
• Better definition for acceptance criteria for tests
• Better end-to-end tests

5   Discussion and Limitations

The aim of this work was to understand which types of debt that require inter-team coordination in LSA by answering the following research question: What types of debt are elicited and discussed on team level and inter-team level in a large-scale agile project?

5.1   What Types of Debt Are Elicited and Discussed on Team Level and Inter-Team Level in a Large-Scale Agile Project?

This study provides an initial source of evidence on the concepts of Technical-, Social and Process Debt, and that inter-team coordination is required to tackle the various types of debt. First, we found that many of the Process Debt issues were re-proposed in the inter-team discussions, which implies that Process Debt needs coordination to be solved, potentially even more than other types of debt. Second, teams discuss heavily Social Debt issues in team retrospectives, and part of the issues are discussed again in large agile retrospectives, especially related to team autonomy, leadership and communication across teams. Third, Technical Debt is discussed in team retrospectives, but only part of it is re-proposed for inter-team discussion.

We did not find Code Debt discussed in retrospectives at all. As for Architecture, Documentation, and Infrastructure, inter-team coordination seems to be necessary when it comes to APIs, documentation used across the teams and the usage of the tools that are used by more teams.

We found a special case related to Test Debt, as some issues were re-proposed (automation, structure), while others were discussed only on a team level. In addition, some of the Test Debt-related issues (e.g. related to acceptance criteria, end-to-end tests) were discussed only on an inter-team level: it seems that such issues were elicited thanks to the joint discussion among teams.

5.2   Limitations and Future Work

In this paper, we used retrospectives to answer our research question. However, other sources of data, for example from other forms of communication, should be analyzed to complement the findings. For example, it could be that architectural issues are discussed in meetings that are more technical rather than in retrospectives. Furthermore, more cases should be analyzed to understand if the results are similar in other large-scale agile projects or if the studied project was a special case.

Acknowledgements. This work was partially supported by the Research Council of Norway through grant 267704 and by the companies Kantega, Knowit, Storebrand and Sbanken.

References

1. Alves, N.S.R., et al.: Towards an ontology of terms on technical debt. In: 2014 Sixth International Workshop on Managing Technical Debt, pp. 1–7 (2014). https://doi.org/10.1109/MTD.2014.9
2. Avgeriou, P., et al.: Managing technical debt in software engineering (dagstuhl seminar 16162). In: Dagstuhl Reports. Schloss Dagstuhl-Leibniz-Zentrum fuer Informatik (2016)
3. Bass, J.M.: Scrum master activities: process tailoring in large enterprise projects. In: 2014 IEEE 9th International Conference on Global Software Engineering, pp. 6–15. IEEE (2014)
4. Cunningham, W.: The WyCash portfolio management system. In: ACM SIGPLAN OOPS Messenger, pp. 29–30. ACM (1992)

5. Dingsøyr, T., et al.: Exploring software development at the very large-scale: a revelatory case study and research agenda for agile method adaptation. Empirical Softw. Eng. **23**(1), 490–520 (2018)
6. Dingsøyr, T., Mikalsen, M., Solem, A., Vestues, K.: Learning in the large - an exploratory study of retrospectives in large-scale agile development. In: Garbajosa, J., Wang, X., Aguiar, A. (eds.) XP 2018. LNBIP, vol. 314, pp. 191–198. Springer, Cham (2018). https://doi.org/10.1007/978-3-319-91602-6_13
7. Kniberg, H.: Scrum and XP from the Trenches. Lulu. com (2015)
8. Li, Z., et al.: A systematic mapping study on technical debt and its management. J. Syst. Soft. **101**, 193–220 (2015). https://doi.org/10.1016/j.jss.2014.12.027
9. Österberg, M., Esni, B., Rabiee, S., Majkowska, Z.: Spotify Retro kit (2017)
10. Moe, N.B., et al.: To schedule or not to schedule? an investigation of meetings as an inter-team coordination mechanism in large-scale agile software development. IJISPM **6**(3), 45–59 (2018)
11. Nyrud, H., Stray, V.: Inter-team coordination mechanisms in large-scale agile. In: Proceedings of the XP2017 Scientific Workshops, pp. 1–6. ACM Press (2017). https://doi.org/10.1145/3120459.3120476
12. Caroli, P., Caetano, T.: Fun retrospectives: activities and ideas for making agile retrospectives more engaging. http://www.caroli.org/product/fun-retrospectives-activities-and-ideas-for-making-agile-retrospectives-more-engaging/
13. Petersen, K., Wohlin, C.: The effect of moving from a plan-driven to an incremental software development approach with agile practices. Empirical Softw. Eng. **15**(6), 654–693 (2010)
14. Stray, V., et al.: Autonomous agile teams: challenges and future directions for research. In: 19th International Conference on Agile Software Development: Companion, XP 2018. ACM, New York (2018). https://doi.org/10.1145/3234152.3234182
15. Stray, V., et al.: Daily stand-up meetings: start breaking the rules. IEEE Software. (2018). https://doi.org/10.1109/MS.2018.2875988
16. Tamburri, D.A., et al.: What is social debt in software engineering? In: 2013 6th International Workshop on Cooperative and Human Aspects of Software Engineering (CHASE), pp. 93–96. IEEE (2013)
17. Version One: 12th State of Agile Report. https://www.infoq.com/news/2018/04/state-of-agile-published
18. Yin, R.K.: Case Study Research: Design and Methods. Sage, Thousand Oaks (2009)

Open Access This chapter is licensed under the terms of the Creative Commons Attribution 4.0 International License (http://creativecommons.org/licenses/by/4.0/), which permits use, sharing, adaptation, distribution and reproduction in any medium or format, as long as you give appropriate credit to the original author(s) and the source, provide a link to the Creative Commons license and indicate if changes were made.

The images or other third party material in this chapter are included in the chapter's Creative Commons license, unless indicated otherwise in a credit line to the material. If material is not included in the chapter's Creative Commons license and your intended use is not permitted by statutory regulation or exceeds the permitted use, you will need to obtain permission directly from the copyright holder.

Doctoral Symposium

Coordination in Large-Scale Agile Software Development

Marthe Berntzen(✉) (iD)

Department of Informatics, University of Oslo, Gaustadalléen 23B,
0730 Oslo, Norway
marthenb@ifi.uio.no

Abstract. Agile practices are popular within software development. But when applied to large projects with many teams, coordination challenges arise. The projects working title "*Coordination in large-scale agile software development: An investigation of coordination mechanisms, communication, roles, autonomy and interdependencies*" summarizes the main topics of investigation. While all theoretical and analytical approaches to the data material is not yet determined, I have already started fieldwork in one company which will serve as a main longitudinal case, with more to follow as the project proceeds. Initial fieldwork has revealed that there are differences in how agile teams coordinate their work across teams. I will continue to explore these differences. End goals of the project include to identify success criteria for coordination in large-scale agile software development projects.

Keywords: Large-scale agile · Software development · Coordination

1 Introduction

The main objective of this PhD project is to contribute to successful software development projects in the digital age, through contributing to a better understanding of coordination in large-scale agile software development projects. There is a recognized need for more research on how to adjust agile practices to large-scale contexts [1–4]. In particular, there is a need for more knowledge on coordination in autonomous agile teams in large-scale settings [3, 5, 6]. Here, I have the opportunity to study large-scale agile projects in a Scandinavian context, where companies seek inspiration from companies like Spotify and Ericsson.

This paper is organized as follows: Sect. 2 outlines some of the relevant background and related work on large-scale agile software development as well as some theoretical approaches to coordination. In Sects. 3 and 4 I present my preliminary research objectives and research design, while Sect. 5 outlines the next planned steps for the research project.

© The Author(s) 2019
R. Hoda (Ed.): XP 2019 Workshops, LNBIP 364, pp. 123–133, 2019.
https://doi.org/10.1007/978-3-030-30126-2_15

2 Background and Relevant Work

2.1 Large-Scale Agile Software Development

Agile teams are autonomous and cross-functional in nature, where team members are assumed to make their own decisions and utilize their competence across different organizational functions and roles. This is thought to contribute to a flatter organizational structure with increased empowerment and participation, assumed to contribute to more efficient decision-making [6–9].

Despite that agile methods originally were intended for smaller team projects [10], and primarily has been successful in small teams [3], the practice of using agile principles and techniques has spread to include large-scale projects and organizations as a whole [9, 11]. At the same time, the research community on agile software development called out the need for a unified framework for understanding large-scale agile software development [12]. As a response to this, a taxonomy of scale for agile software projects was developed, where small-scale agile software development includes one team only, large-scale from 2–9 teams, and very large-scale from 10 teams and up [12].

When scaling up agile, several challenges arise, such as coordination between teams, stakeholder management and keeping to the agile principles [1, 3, 5]. One challenge with applying agile to large-scale is that there is a lack of a common, agreed upon understanding of agile working methods [13]. Rather, agile can be understood as a set of values, principles and practices, that may be implemented in more or less successful ways. As such, there may be great differences in how large-scale agile is implemented [14], and finding consistent results from large-scale agile may be difficult [13]. Initial fieldwork supports these observations. In Berntzen et al. [15] we discuss how differences in Product Owner coordination may be related to that teams in the large-scale case program under study may freely choose among agile methods, in other words, they do not work consistently with one agile approach.

Another challenge is related to how large-scale frameworks, such as the Spotify model, Large-Scale Scrum and the Scaled Agile Framework may affect large-scale coordination. Such frameworks are gaining in popularity, but there is still a need for more academic research on such practices, as there is little research supporting that agile principles can be directly applied to all organizational processes without adjustment or tailoring [1, 14, 16].

Among the many challenges inherent in the successful implementation of large-scale agile coordination appears to be a key issue. Dikert et al. [1] identify inter-team coordination as one of the major challenges in need of more research. Coordination, often defined as the managing of interdependencies [17] is recognized as important across literatures on software engineering, information systems, organization and management [26], and theories on coordination has been developed [4, 17]. While researchers have started exploring coordination in large-scale agile [1–3, 5, 16, 18, 19], there are still many open questions in need for further investigations.

2.2   Coordination Theories

Coordination Theory

Malone and Crowston [17] developed an interdisciplinary, broad-based theory of coordination, known today as Coordination Theory (CT). In their seminal paper, Malone and Crowston [17, p. 4] defined coordination as a process of "managing dependencies between activities". CT is based on ideas from organization theory, management, economics and computer science [4]. The basic tenet of CT is that complex organizational systems are made up of dependencies (such as shared resources, task interdependencies, simultaneity constraints and relationships with clients, each with different sub-dependencies), which constrain situational action, and thus must be coordinated. Coordination then, is made up by various coordination processes and mechanisms which each address one or more dependencies in a situation [17]. What these processes and mechanisms are and how they work vary with the context. In the context of large-scale agile software development, they can include for instance scheduled and unscheduled meetings, artefacts and physical settings [4, 20]. These mechanisms may facilitate action constrained by the dependencies, however, the in the large-scale setting, perhaps the mechanisms themselves may also both enable and constrain coordinated action?

CT has contributed with a much-cited definition of coordination, a modelling framework for analyzing coordination in complex processes and providing a beginning of a typology of dependencies and coordination mechanisms [21]. However, it does not provide any propositions or testable hypotheses [17, 21]. In a ten-year retrospective of CT research, future research to develop testable hypotheses from CT is encouraged, for instance about the generality of coordination mechanisms and more structured approaches to evaluate alternate coordination processes [21].

Despite the limitations of the theory in terms of lack of causal explanations and testable hypotheses, CT has proved a useful theoretical framework for the study of coordination. In the IS field, CT has been used in particular in software engineering and systems design, where researchers have noted the importance of coordination challenges and the potential for computer systems to help groups and teams collaborate better [21]. In the context of agile software development, CT has been applied by Strode and colleagues [4], who used the theory as basis for their own development of a theory of coordination in agile development.

The Theory of Coordination in Agile Development

To take advance theory and research on coordination in agile SD further, Strode and colleagues [4] build on Coordination theory but extended with a theoretical model and a total of eight testable propositions. In particular, this theory proposes that effective coordination in agile settings are comprised of coordination strategies contributing to coordination effectiveness. Coordination strategies are defined as a group of coordination mechanisms that manage dependencies in a situation. They consist of three components; synchronization, structure and boundary spanning activities and artefacts that contribute to overall coordination effectiveness [4].

Coordination effectiveness, in turn, consists of explicit and implicit effectiveness. Explicit coordination effectiveness emphasizes the physical objects (both persons and artefacts) involved in the project. For *explicit coordination effectiveness* to occur, the required object needs to be in the right place, at the right time and in the right state so that is "ready for use" as perceived by each individual involved in the project [4, 17]. Having the right tools in place to conduct a video meeting or having available developers to take on new tasks as they flow from a different team can be examples of this type of explicit coordination effectiveness. *Implicit coordination effectiveness* on the other hand, relates to coordination that occurs within work groups without explicit passing of messages. The authors further posit that implicit coordination consists of five components; "knowing why", "knowing what is going on and when", "knowing what to do and when", "knowing who is doing what" and "knowing who knows what". In other words, implicit coordination requires a high degree of shared goals and understanding both of one's own and others knowledge [4]. In relation to agile development, where the team is central [22], implicit coordination in terms of shared knowledge indeed appears important to overall project effectiveness.

Importantly, in this theory, these are considered outcomes resulting from the coordination strategy. The theoretical model proposes that there is a causal relationship between an agile coordination strategy and project coordination effectiveness; if the strategies are well implemented, coordination is more effective. This in turn, is proposed to contribute to the agile software development project success [4]. In addition, they propose that project complexity, uncertainty and organization structure may affect the coordination strategies, but they did not test this while developing the theory.

Despite its clear relevant to the study of coordination in agile development, this theory is difficult to readily apply it my PhD project because it considers *intra-team* coordination and does not consider the multiple team aspect and *inter-team* coordination, which may introduce important constraints to effective coordination. In order to apply their theoretical model to large-scale agile development, it could be necessary to expand the model to include elements such as for instance team size, number of teams, number of functional elements involved in the project as well as differences in team autonomy in their usage of agile methods and choice of technologies across teams. Accordingly, one route may be to further develop the theory to account for scale. Another route is to look further into theories that may take into account the multiple team aspect, and the various differences these entail, through focusing on the coordination process itself through a relational lens.

Relational Coordination Theory

Relational Coordination Theory (RCT) [23] represents a third theoretical perspective on coordination. RCT originates in the organization studies field from research conducted in the airline industry in the 1990s [23], where Gittell observed substantial difference between companies in the extent to which the employees shared collective goals and knowledge towards the overall work process and outcome. Today, RCT is an established and empirically validated theory, and has been studied in various (non-agile)

large-scale settings, most notably in the airplane, health and education industries [24][1].
RCT has recently been picked up by Information Systems researchers [25–27], however, it appears it has not yet been applied in large-scale agile development.

Relational coordination is defined as "a mutually reinforcing process of interaction
between communication and relationships carried out for the purpose of task integration" [28]. These relationships can be between individuals, roles or even departments
and organizations. According to RCT, relationships provide the necessary bandwidth
for coordinating work in settings with that are highly interdependent, uncertain and
time-constrained. Effective coordination in these settings is carried out through relationships of shared goals, shared knowledge and mutual respect. These, in turn, are
theorized to be mutually reinforced by high-quality communication (that is, frequent,
timely, accurate and problem-solving communication). It is interesting to note that
these assumptions bears resemblance to Strode et al.'s implicit coordination effectiveness [4] described in the above section. The resulting positive relational context
enables a well-coordinated process with less wasted effort [23]. Finally, an assumption
of RCT is that relational coordination has is stronger in more horizontally designed
organizational structures [29]. Because large-scale agile software development processes are also typically characterized by high levels of interdependence, uncertainty
and time pressure, in combination with other coordination theories, I believe RCT is an
interesting lens for studying coordination in large-scale agile development.

Further Theoretical Considerations
Although the above presented theories all can contribute to the understanding of
coordination processes in large-scale agile, it is still necessary to focus not only on the
social and human aspects of coordination, but also the role of the product under
development and the technologies being used during the development.

All three coordination theories offer some concepts that address coordination in
large-scale agile development, however the role of large-scale itself, as well as the
potential implications of both the technology being used for coordination, and the
technology being developed is perhaps not fully addressed. In order to fully accom-
modate these theories to be relevant for large-scale agile development, and to make
valuable theoretical contributions to IS and SE fields, it may be relevant to draw on
other theories and concepts. As one overarching project goal is to address how coordination mechanisms are used in and across teams, and as initial fieldwork has indicated that teams in large-scale agile projects coordinate differently [15], it is important
to address how different coordination mechanisms may be used in different ways. To
this end, I believe that other theories and concepts from the IS field, such as
sociotechnical systems perspectives, affordance theory [30] and/or the concept of
boundary objects [31] could help me understand how teams go about using agile
practices and tools differently, depending on their needs and goals, and how this in
turn, may reinforce differences through the different action possibilities offered by e.g.
technological communication tools, meetings and physical artefacts used in agile
activities [32].

---

[1] A full overview of research results from this line of research is beyond the scope of this paper. See
for instance [24], an overview of research and future directions of RCT.

Getting the theory right is a substantial task in a PhD project, and a task I will direct much attention to in the time to come. However, as I will continue to explore how RCT may inform my research project, I will explore recent literature combining RCT with approaches taking into account the role of the technology itself. For instance, Clagett and Karahanna [26] explore the role of relational coordination in digitally mediated work processes and focus in particular on distributed information exchanges for dependency management and the role of boundary spanners in facilitating digitally mediated coordination. Bozan [25] applied RCT in an empirical investigation of collaboration and creative group problem solving in a virtual, distributed team environment and found that RCT's elements of high-quality relationships and high-quality communication did have a positive impact on creative problem-solving in distributed teams.

In the further development of my PhD project, I will look into these and other theoretical approaches to identify the best suited approach to understanding coordination in large-scale settings.

3 Research Objectives and Preliminary Research Questions

The main objective of the project includes identifying success criteria for coordination, such as how to handle interdependencies, enable good communication and better autonomous team-work processes in large-scale agile software development projects. The final output will be a dissertation in the form of an article collection with conference and journal papers.

To gain more understanding about the topics outlined above, I will explore in a field setting research questions such as:

- How are coordination mechanisms used in and across large-scale agile software development projects?
- How do Product Owners coordinate work in large-scale agile software development [15]?
- Which interdependencies operates in and across teams in agile software development projects and what challenges do they pose for team efficiency?
- What is the role of written communication in large-scale agile coordination?

Some of these research questions may be too broad in their current form. Therefore, they will be reworked as the empirical studies are conducted.

4 Research Design

To address the research questions, I primarily plan to use qualitative research methods in a longitudinal case study. The case study approach was chosen because case studies provide depth and detailed knowledge [33] and there is little research-based knowledge about how POs coordinate work in large-scale agile. Data will be collected in the field from several companies associated with the Autonomous teams-project (A-teams) in collaboration with SINTEF.

The data collection methods will include participant observation, individual and potentially group interviews, document analysis [34] and surveys [35]. Collecting a rich data material that can be analyzed in different ways to gain a broad understanding of the research topic and to address the outlined research questions.

4.1 Case Description

I have conducted field work in a large-scale agile development program, referred to as the PubTrans program, since September 2018. The data so far has been collected from a large-scale case in which almost the whole development program is co-located and working with agile development methods. The program started in 2016 and aims to develop a new platform supporting public transportation.

The PubTrans program has thirteen development teams ranging between five and fourteen team members working toward developing the same products. Each team is responsible for their part of the overall product. The PubTrans program can thus be classified as very large-scale agile [12, 36]. In order to coordinate work within and across teams, the program makes use of various electronic tools, such as Slack, Jira, and Confluence; material artefacts such as task boards; and various scheduled and unscheduled meetings. The development teams may choose freely how they solve their tasks and may rely on agile methods of choice. As such, there is no one unified agile approach across the teams.

I spend 1–2 days a week there, observing how they work and attend in particular inter-team meetings. In addition, twelve interviews were conducted in October 2018, with a focus on the Product Owner role, and one interview with a team leader was conducted April 2019. More interviews, with more roles, are planned the coming fall. In addition, I have access to a wide range of written documentation, including Slack logs, Confluence pages and company wiki.

Based on the data collected so far, one conference paper has been presented and published [15]. This paper explores through an RCT lens how Product Owners coordinate within and across agile software development teams in a large-scale public sector program in Norway. Data collection in this program will continue throughout the PhD research project, with supplemental data collection in other companies to follow at a later stage.

In addition to my own presence at the PubTrans program site, one of my supervisors are taking an active part in the fieldwork conducted there. In collaboration, we make sure to provide the program with regular feedback and keep them well informed about the research progress. Whenever a paper is written and sent for review, they are given opportunity to review and approve the data used and results presented, and are offered opportunities to contribute also in terms of co-authoring. Nurturing a good relationship with the case organization is seen as highly valuable for both parties.

All in all, the PubTrans program proves an increasingly valuable case to work with. My access to data is good, and the processes and changes we observe them doing proves interesting and worthwhile of continuous focus. Initially, I planned to include at least three company cases, devoting approximately the same amount of time and efforts to each of them. However, over the past months I have decided that the PubTrans program should serve as the main case for a longitudinal, in-depth case study which can provide rich empirical insights into the research topic [33].

Despite the advantages of longitudinal case studies, there is an inherent trade-off in terms of potential lack of generalizability to other companies and settings [33, 37]. Here, researchers need to weigh the benefits and disadvantages against each other in making a decision. As one means to improve generalizability to other settings, towards the end of the data collection, I will collect supplemental data from other companies I have access to. This data collection will not be as detailed as that of the PubTrans program, however it may serve to cross-check some of the observations and findings into other settings to see if there are great similarities or differences from the PubTrans program to other settings. Of course, no two organizations are alike, so differences are likely to observed. Nevertheless, it is thought worthwhile to do such additional data collection to strengthen my findings.

4.2 Validity Issues and How to Address Them

In terms of validity, which threats and how to control them depends on the research method. For qualitative methods, researcher bias is important to address. I intend to rely on data triangulation, using both interviews, observation and document analysis. Triangulation generate more substantial data, addressing the topics under study from different angels [33]. Further, the analysis of the qualitative data material will involve textual coding. I will use programs such as Nvivo 12 for organizing the codes and conducting the analyses, however, bias and validity threats are prevalent when coding data. Own preconceptions on behalf of the researcher and fatigue are only two of these threats. Further, as much of the analyses will be conducted at least partly in collaboration with others, I will make sure to assess the inter-rater reliability for the analyses to try to assure coding reliability and validity. My supervisors have strong expertise in qualitative research methods, and they will help me ensure validity is sufficiently addressed.

5   Current Research Status and Next Planned Steps

This research project is still in an early phase, and despite the encouraging outset, much remains to be done. In this section, I will describe some of the outstanding issues that should be clarified as I proceed with the research project.

First, the literature on agile software development is already substantial, and the literature on large-scale agile is growing. As I continue to go through these bodies of literatures, I will conduct a literature review to gain a fuller overview of the current state of research on coordination in large-scale agile software development. Here, examining both research papers and the practitioner literature may be a worthwhile endeavor, as there is a substantial practitioner literature within this field.

Second, I will work further on the scope of my research, as it is still somewhat too broad. This includes further delineating the theoretical approaches as well as narrowing down the focus of my research questions. While I will continue exploring the usability of RCT as a theoretical lens for understanding coordination in large-scale agile, I will need to pin down how theory can inform my understanding of how technologies used during development, as well as the product under development, affects coordination.

Finally, I am already planning to collect enough data to allow me to carry on with my research also after the completion of the PhD research project. As described above in Sect. 4, I plan to collect survey data that can be analyzed quantitatively. Much research in the SE field and on large-scale agile is qualitative, which makes it interesting to see whether quantitative research can bring new insights. I have an interest in both types of research. Before starting my PhD, I have also conducted quantitative research based on surveys from another research project. These studies explore distributed, autonomous teams in relation to their coordination under conditions of different levels of initiated and received task interdependence [38] and in relation to how distributed team members perceive certain leadership styles [39]. Continuing such lines of research in a large-scale agile setting could be an interesting future research project.

However, as it can be argued that qualitative studies are more suitable when exploring new grounds [33], I will conduct qualitative research for the PhD project and potentially supplement with quantitative studies at a later stage in my career. In conclusion, doing research on coordination in large-scale agile software development is an exciting endeavor. Many challenges lie ahead as this PhD project continues; however, I remain optimistic about the future and look forward to tackling these challenges as they unfold.

References

1. Dikert, K., Paasivaara, M., Lassenius, C.: Challenges and success factors for large-scale agile transformations: a systematic literature review. J. Syst. Softw. **119**, 87–108 (2016). https://doi.org/10.1016/j.jss.2016.06.013
2. Dingsøyr, T., Moe, N.B.: Research challenges in large-scale agile software development. ACM SIGSOFT Softw. Eng. Not. **38**, 38–39 (2013)
3. Dingsøyr, T., Moe, N.B.: Towards principles of large-scale agile development. In: Dingsøyr, T., Moe, N.B., Tonelli, R., Counsell, S., Gencel, C., Petersen, K. (eds.) XP 2014. LNBIP, vol. 199, pp. 1–8. Springer, Cham (2014). https://doi.org/10.1007/978-3-319-14358-3_1
4. Strode, D.E., Huff, S.L., Hope, B., Link, S.: Coordination in co-located agile software development projects. J. Syst. Softw. **85**, 1222–1238 (2012). https://doi.org/10.1016/j.jss.2012.02.017
5. Dingsøyr, T., Moe, N.B., Seim, E.A.: Coordinating knowledge work in multi-team programs: findings from a large-scale agile development program. Proj. Manag. J. **49**, 64–77 (2018)
6. Lee, G., Xia, W.: Toward agile: an integrated analysis of quantitative and qualitative field data on software development agility. MIS Q. **34**, 87–114 (2010)
7. Moe, N.B., Dingsøyr, T., Dybå, T.: Overcoming barriers to self-management in software teams. IEEE Softw. **26**, 20–26 (2009)
8. Hoda, R., Noble, J., Marshall, S.: Self-organizing roles on agile software development teams. IEEE Trans. Softw. Eng. **39**, 422–444 (2013). https://doi.org/10.1109/TSE.2012.30
9. Hoda, R., Salleh, N., Grundy, J.: The rise and evolution of agile software development. IEEE Softw. **35**, 58–63 (2018). https://doi.org/10.1109/MS.2018.290111318

10. Williams, L., Cockburn, A.: guest editors' introduction: agile software development: it's about feedback and change. Computer **36**, 39–43 (2003)
11. Rigby, D.K., Sutherland, J., Noble, A.: Agile at scale: how to go from a few team to hundreds. Harvard Bus. Rev. **96**, 88–96 (2018)
12. Dingsøyr, T., Nerur, S., Balijepally, V., Moe, N.B.: A decade of agile methodologies: towards explaining agile software development. J. Syst. Softw. **85**, 1213–1221 (2012). https://doi.org/10.1016/j.jss.2012.02.033
13. Jørgensen, M.: Do agile methods work for large software projects? In: Garbajosa, J., Wang, X., Aguiar, A. (eds.) XP 2018. LNBIP, vol. 314, pp. 179–190. Springer, Cham (2018). https://doi.org/10.1007/978-3-319-91602-6_12
14. Paasivaara, M., Behm, B., Lassenius, C., Hallikainen, M.: Large-scale agile transformation at Ericsson: a case study. Empirical Softw. Eng. **23**(5), 2250–2596 (2018)
15. Berntzen, M., Moe, N.B., Stray, V.: The product owner in large-scale agile: an empirical study through the lens of relational coordination theory. In: Kruchten, P., Fraser, S., Coallier, F. (eds.) XP 2019. LNBIP, vol. 355, pp. 121–136. Springer, Cham (2019). https://doi.org/10.1007/978-3-030-19034-7_8
16. Putta, A., Paasivaara, M., Lassenius, C.: Benefits and challenges of adopting the scaled agile framework (SAFe): preliminary results from a multivocal literature review. In: Kuhrmann, M., et al. (eds.) PROFES 2018. LNCS, vol. 11271, pp. 334–351. Springer, Cham (2018). https://doi.org/10.1007/978-3-030-03673-7_24
17. Malone, T.W., Crowston, K.: The interdisciplinary study of coordination. ACM Comput. Surv. (CSUR) **26**, 87–119 (1994)
18. Dingsøyr, T., Bjørnson, F.O., Moe, N.B., Rolland, K., Seim, E.A.: Rethinking coordination in large-scale software development. Presented at the Proceedings of the 11th International Workshop on Cooperative and Human Aspects of Software Engineering (2018)
19. Paasivaara, M., Lassenius, C., Heikkila, V.T.: Inter-team coordination in large-scale globally distributed scrum: do scrum-of-scrums really work? In: Proceedings of the ACM-IEEE International Symposium on Empirical Software Engineering and Measurement, Lund, Sweden (2012)
20. Nyrud, H., Stray, V.: Inter-team coordination mechanisms in large-scale agile. Presented at the Proceedings of the XP2017 Scientific Workshops (2017)
21. Howison, J., Rubleske, J., Crowston, K.: Coordination theory: a ten-year retrospective. In: Human-Computer Interaction and Management Information Systems: Foundations, pp. 134–152. Routledge (2015)
22. Moe, N.B., Dingsøyr, T., Dybå, T.: A teamwork model for understanding an agile team: a case study of a Scrum project. Inf. Softw. Technol. **52**, 480–491 (2010). https://doi.org/10.1016/j.infsof.2009.11.004
23. Gittell, J.H.: Relational coordination: coordinating work through relationships of shared goals, shared knowledge and mutual respect. In: Relational Perspectives in Organizational Studies: A Research Companion, pp. 74–94 (2006)
24. Gittell, J.H.: New directions for relational coordination theory. In: Spreitzer, G.M., Cameron, K.S. (eds.) The Oxford Handbook of Positive Organizational Scholarship. Oxford University Press (2012)
25. Bozan, K.: The perceived level of collaborative work environment's effect on creative group problem solving in a virtual and distributed team environment. Presented at the Proceedings of the 50th Hawaii International Conference on System Sciences (2017)
26. Claggett, J.L., Karahanna, E.: Unpacking the structure of coordination mechanisms and the role of relational coordination in an era of digitally mediated work processes. Acad. Manag. Rev. **43**, 704–722 (2018)

27. Sebastian, I.M., Bui, T.: The influence of IS affordances on work practices in health care: a relational coordination approach. Presented at the International Conference on Information Systems (2012)
28. Gittell, J.H.: Coordinating mechanisms in care provider groups: relational coordination as a mediator and input uncertainty as a moderator of performance effects. Manag. Sci. **48**, 1408–1426 (2002)
29. Gittell, J.H., Douglass, A.: Relational bureaucracy: structuring reciprocal relationships into roles. Acad. Manag. Rev. **37**, 709–733 (2012)
30. Volkoff, O., Strong, D.M.: Affordance theory and how to use it in IS research. In: The Routledge Companion to Management Information Systems. Routledge, New York (2018)
31. Doolin, B., McLeod, L.: Sociomateriality and boundary objects in information systems development. Eur. J. Inf. Syst. **21**, 570–586 (2012). https://doi.org/10.1057/ejis.2012.20
32. Leonardi, P.M.: When flexible routines meet flexible technologies: affordance, constraint, and the imbrication of human and material agencies. MIS Q. **35**, 147–167 (2011)
33. Yin, R.K.: Case Study Research and Applications: Design and Methods. Sage Publications, Thousand Oaks (2018)
34. Crang, M., Cook, I.: Doing Ethnographies. Sage, Thousand Oaks (2007)
35. Alreck, P.L., Settle, R.B.: The Survey Research Handbook. McGraw-Hill, New York (1994)
36. Dingsøyr, T., Moe, N.B., Fægri, T.E., Seim, E.A.: Exploring software development at the very large-scale: a revelatory case study and research agenda for agile method adaptation. Empirical Softw. Eng. 1–31 (2017). https://doi.org/10.1007/s10664-017-9524-2
37. Diefenbach, T.: Are case studies more than sophisticated storytelling?: Methodological problems of qualitative empirical research mainly based on semi-structured interviews. Qual. Quant. **43**, 875 (2009)
38. Berntzen, M., Wong, S.I.: Coordination in distributed, self-managing work teams: the roles of initiated and received task interdependence. In: Proceedings of the 52nd Hawaii International Conference on System Sciences (2019)
39. Wong, S.I., Berntzen, M.: Transformational leadership and leader–member exchange in distributed teams: the roles of electronic dependence and team task interdependence. Comput. Hum. Behav. **92**, 381–392 (2019). https://doi.org/10.1016/j.chb.2018.11.032

Open Access This chapter is licensed under the terms of the Creative Commons Attribution 4.0 International License (http://creativecommons.org/licenses/by/4.0/), which permits use, sharing, adaptation, distribution and reproduction in any medium or format, as long as you give appropriate credit to the original author(s) and the source, provide a link to the Creative Commons license and indicate if changes were made.

The images or other third party material in this chapter are included in the chapter's Creative Commons license, unless indicated otherwise in a credit line to the material. If material is not included in the chapter's Creative Commons license and your intended use is not permitted by statutory regulation or exceeds the permitted use, you will need to obtain permission directly from the copyright holder.

Panels

XP 2019 Panel: Security and Privacy

Dennis Mancl[1]([⊠]) [iD] and Steven D. Fraser[2] [iD]

[1] MSWX Software Experts, Bridgewater, NJ 08807, USA
dmancl@acm.org
[2] Innoxec, Santa Clara, CA, USA
sdfraser@acm.org

Abstract. In reaction to reports of recent high-profile software security and privacy failures in our always-on agile world, users and regulators are demanding that companies deliver more trustworthy and resilient systems. This panel discussed some of the strategies and best practices for "building-in security" to our products and systems in contrast to "bolting-on security" – and how threats should be assessed and mitigated to avoid the unintended consequences of flawed design decisions.

Keywords: Security · Privacy · Design

1 Security and Privacy at XP 2019

Security and privacy issues for today's computer systems and applications are in the headlines. Every day there are business stories about companies who lose customer data to hackers, stories about system outages caused by hackers, and stories about shadowy networks of criminals who take over computers and blackmail helpless companies, governments, and ordinary users. The panel discussion on security and privacy issues was motivated by the special challenges to building software systems in an agile way: even in a lightweight development process, all developers still need to pay attention to software quality, security from hackers, and protection of the private data of users.

The panel represented a cross section of industry experience in software applications. Landon Noll is a computer security expert, astronomer, and frequent traveler to the South Pole. He currently works for Cisco in California. Kelsey van Haaster is a software engineering expert at ThoughtWorks Australia who works on her company's internal security practices: passwords, security hygiene, and identity-related issues. Scott Ambler is a consultant, coach, and author of books on object-oriented design and Agile development methods, and he is currently Senior Consulting Partner at Scott Ambler + Associates based in Canada. Dennis Mancl worked as an internal software engineering and software quality expert at AT&T and Lucent in New Jersey. Robert Crawhall is a Principal Consultant at Innoxec in Ottawa, Ontario, where he developed technologies for government and industry, including nuclear power and telecom systems. Steven Fraser, the panel impresario, is based in California where he advises on tech transfer and open innovation strategies for Innoxec. Previously he was the Director of the Cisco Research Center and the Lead for HP's Global University Programs – and he has organized and delivered over 75 software engineering conferences, panels, and workshops.

© The Author(s) 2019
R. Hoda (Ed.): XP 2019 Workshops, LNBIP 364, pp. 137–142, 2019.
https://doi.org/10.1007/978-3-030-30126-2_16

2 Security and Privacy Panel Discussion

Agile development creates special challenges in developing software systems that appropriately address security and privacy.

In this panel, the following issues were raised by the panelists: Security design should cover prevention, mitigation, and detection of security issues. Good "security hygiene" is an important practice for all software designers and developers. Many of our devices today are inherently insecure, and we need to be aware of the risks as we design our systems. In any development effort, especially in a fast-paced Agile development cycle, it is important to identify the security requirements up front and always include these requirements in the test planning and execution. Today's developers need to address more government regulations on security and privacy. In an Agile environment, customers need to be made aware of security tradeoffs. In addition, there is a significant "training gap" in security and privacy training.

Landon Noll started the discussion by asserting that we can never be perfect at preventing security and privacy issues in our software. We should try to prevent security problems when we can, but whatever we can't prevent we should try to mitigate, and whatever we can't mitigate we should at least try to detect.

Landon explained that testing, logging, and monitoring are the most important security-related practices and tools for development teams. Development teams need to think about security tests up front, and the teams need to have a process to continuously improve tests as the team learns more. An Agile development approach is valuable because it supports continuous improvement. Landon explained the value of Agile's focus on improvement, "I think Agile process gives you a really good way to be in this continuous process of improving your testing, testing your improvements, measuring your improvements, measuring the logging, and logging the measurement."

But there is no silver bullet for security and privacy. Landon warned about some of the risks of our current security technology. Many of our security technologies are inadequate. Landon pointed out, for example, "We demand too much from hash functions – more than they can deliver." He complained that many of our security standards say "use this cryptographic hash function," but the best hash functions "are being attacked faster than Moore's Law." Cryptographic hash functions are at the heart of authentication and communications security systems, including digital signatures and public key cryptography [1]. Landon concluded that designers of most secure systems don't pay enough attention to important activities in using encryption tools, such as key generation and key management.

Kelsey van Haaster emphasized the importance of good security hygiene. In her company, security is everyone's concern. "At ThoughtWorks, we ensure that every consultant (whether they are a software developer or a business analyst or a project manager) goes through our App Sec 101 training. When we are working with clients and building products, both for clients and internally, we take the approach that the security stories need to be there from iteration zero. We build that into part of our process right from the start."

Scott Ambler and Landon Noll told some cautionary tales about the theft of information from our computers and devices.

Scott had security and privacy anecdotes from his days working for IBM where some global customers of IBM would routinely try to steal data from visiting outsiders. His colleagues in the IBM sales organization knew which companies were "bad actors," and they would warn him, "Don't bring your phone and laptop to this customer site." They suspected that even an encrypted hard drive could be vulnerable.

Landon reported about the deficiencies of today's hardware: "The overall state of computer hardware is somewhere between appallingly poor and unacceptably poor." Every computer is vulnerable if a hacker finds a way to load and execute small selected chunks of code. According to Landon, "All commercially available microprocessors today are subject to having their integrity compromised by a sequence of non-privileged instructions." This is bad news for digital security for applications such as containers, virtual machines, IoT, and cloud computing.

Dennis Mancl advocated for the importance of security requirements – which need to be part of the requirements documentation even in Agile development projects. "Security requirements are really important, because if you are going to test a system, what are you going to test it against? If there are no security requirements, they don't care about it."

The ITU-T X.805 security architecture recommendations include a set of eight security dimensions, and every system needs to have some security requirements in each area [2]. The security dimensions are linked to potential security risks, threats, and vulnerabilities. Access control and authentication requirements specify the rules for physical and network access to a system and the rules for application and network passwords. Non-repudiation requirements explain the transaction records and logs that must be maintained to allow stakeholders to prove that an event took place. Data confidentiality and communications security requirements ensure that data is kept private. Data integrity requirements describe the internal system processes to prevent data from unauthorized duplication or modification. Availability requirements define the responses to system overload and to denial of service attacks. Privacy requirements prevent disclosure of information about users' network communications activities, such as the IP address of a user or websites the user has visited.

Security requirements are not easy to write. When writing security requirements, it helps to consult with experienced testers. Testers can give constructive suggestions for key security requirements to include in requirements documents or user stories, based on the testers' experiences with security testing for similar systems.

Security analysis often needs to focus on "negative" behavior. Many security requirements are "misuse cases" – key scenarios that explain what things need to be prevented or mitigated. In Agile development, too many of the user stories written by developers and users are unrealistically positive: most of them are "the system acts nice" stories. It is a good idea to get together with friends who are testers when doing user story brainstorming, because testers are better trained to think about negative cases.

There are many new security and privacy regulations in place, such as the European Union's General Data Protection Regulation (GDPR), which was put into effect in 2018. Robert Crawhall explained the pressures on governments to create new security regulations.

Robert agreed that governments really want commercial computer systems to be more secure and private, but "government has a very limited toolbox." Their standards are intended to improve focus on certain issues by companies. "When the government gets to control the supply chain, they start implementing standards to try and cover their butts." This explains complex standards like the GDPR privacy rules. It is impossible for governments to catch every violation of the new security or privacy regulations, but they can make an example of a few big companies who don't follow the rules. "If you're the European Union, you bring in GPDR for the same reason – and you hope that handing out a few $5 billion fines will cause industry to sit up and take notice."

Some of the audience members added their own observations. "Today, I got an email request from where I work – telling me to log in using my credentials to do security training on how not to click bait in email." Landon was interested: "Did you do the training?" "No, of course not."

The same audience member had another complaint about the effect of GDPR on application interfaces. Users are asked to agree to allow access in the middle of an application, and this access permission process is extremely superficial. "I would suggest that GDPR makes us significantly less secure and private than we have ever been. Because to access anything, no matter what it is, you have to say 'Yes, I agree'. So all of a sudden, we are giving permission on purpose to access data, and we are not reading all of the levels of permission we are giving."

One question from the audience explained the problems of getting customers to be interested in security. "Often your customer – when you do work for a large company and they have a Product Owner for an Agile project – they want their features. So they find it hard to prioritize security." Even if the customer understands the need for some good security hygiene and some up-front analysis of security issues, it can be easy for them to put a lower priority on adding new security functionality to face new threats. Some customers are just hard to convince that they should invest in security prevention and attack analysis.

Kelsey explained how at ThoughtWorks, the teams actively include businesspeople in the project inception process – the early discussions where security scenarios and other iteration zero tasks are planned. She explained, "They don't need to get involved in the technical details, but there is always a financial or a business or a reputational risk that those folks care about."

Robert commented that a company needs strong accountability and transparency in its decision-making process. Early in his career, he worked on the design of nuclear power plants, and the "signoff" process ensured that engineers took quality seriously. "In a 40-year engineering career, the one day I still remember is when I put my stamp on the design of a nuclear pressure vessel, with implications for northern Ontario if I made a mistake on the calculations."

Strong oversight can also help. Robert explained that in his experience in the development of nuclear power plants, the ultimate yes/no decisions on all quality-related issues were signed off by the "head of quality" for the company, who reported directly to the CEO. If a decision went wrong, it was clear who was responsible.

Scott and Robert reported on aspects of customer apathy and ignorance. Scott pointed out the inevitability of customer apathy: "The problem is you're fighting human nature. It's human nature not to think about bad things." He talked about how many people build houses in river floodplains or in coastal areas vulnerable to hurricanes. And Robert pointed out the differences between the layout of the original

Canadian telephone trunk network and the design of the internet exchange network a generation later. The main east-west trunks of the older telephone networks went 45 miles north of Toronto: "if they lost Toronto, they didn't want to lose the telephone connection between Montreal and Calgary." But in the 1990s, Bell Canada chose to install their main Toronto internet exchange in downtown Toronto in the One Front St. building, at street level, subject to flooding and perhaps vulnerable to a terrorist attack. Robert comment was "it's because it became deregulated."

One questioner lamented the lack of education in digital security issues and suggested that security training needs to start in elementary schools. "At what point should we teach software developers how code is compromised based on data, and proven practices to avoid those compromises?... in all of my time and all of my education since I started teaching at the undergraduate level in 1971, I have never seen a course teach this." If no one learns about digital security issues, developers will continue to build systems with weak security.

Robert and Landon suggested that teaching about digital security ought to be done when middle schoolers or elementary school students first learn about programming.

Robert explained that as part of the Cyber New Brunswick initiative, the schools in the Canadian province of New Brunswick now all include cyber security concepts in the middle school curriculum. Robert explains, "They need to catch kids before they make the STEM/not-STEM decision."

Landon explained that it is important for young people to learn to think about what can go wrong. He offered his experience in teaching security thinking at kids camps: "I get them to do something simple like print 'Hi mom.' Then I ask 'How can you mess it up?' One clever girl, she thought a little bit, then she went over and turned off the computer." Once you have figured out how to mess something up, "you need to think about how to fix that messing up," and then go back and forth with the students. "They learn that they maybe need to save their work." It starts them thinking about how to analyze problems.

Scott explained that the education and training gap about security is part of a bigger problem. "When are we going to start teaching people to code/program? Forget asking when we're going to teach programmers how to be secure, when are we going to ask our people to have adequate educations? I work in banks and insurance companies, and most of the developers in the IT space don't have a background in programming. They don't have the fundamental skills of their jobs."

Scott explained that we would be making the same comments in a panel on User Experience or Performance, because there are similar gaps in knowledge and experience across industry in those areas.

Kelsey pointed out that companies can play a role by putting computer security resources in the hands every employee and their families. "We provide every employee with a family subscription for a password manager, and we insist that they in fact use it." Kelsey points out that this can save money: "it is cheaper than something going horribly wrong." This is a policy that can have a positive long-term impact: "Kids of our employees are growing up understanding about their own personal security."

3 Summary

Security and privacy will continue to be important issues to address for Agile development. The panelists all warned about the gap between security threats and the current security technologies. They pointed out the deficiencies in software development training – not enough focus on what can go wrong. In a corporate environment, security is everyone's concern and all developers and users need to practice good security hygiene. It is essential to document the security requirements in the course of developing a system. Some security and privacy standards, such as the GDPR privacy rules, may actually create new security and privacy risks. There can be a disconnect between the development teams and the Product Owner about the relative value of work items that improve an application's security infrastructure. Finally, everyone needs some encouragement and training in security and privacy issues: something as simple as a company-provided family subscription for a password manager can improve the awareness of good security practices.

Landon summarized the main message about security and privacy for the audience: "Train early. Test often." He concluded with a message of Agile improvement: An Agile process supports "continuously improving your testing, testing your improvements, measuring your improvements, measuring the logging, logging the measurement." Small group of developers can "go off and try to see if they can break something, and figure out how to mitigate that." It's a process that requires new software to be tested early: "and continue testing from the foundations, as your code needs to work – and to work correctly – with the reliability, privacy, and integrity that you need."

References

1. Chi, L., Zhu, X.: Hashing techniques. ACM Comput. Surv. **50**(1), 1–36 (2017). https://doi.org/10.1145/3047307
2. International Telecommunications Union (2003): ITU-T X.805 Security architecture for systems providing end-to-end communications. https://www.itu.int/rec/T-REC-X.805-200310-I

Open Access This chapter is licensed under the terms of the Creative Commons Attribution 4.0 International License (http://creativecommons.org/licenses/by/4.0/), which permits use, sharing, adaptation, distribution and reproduction in any medium or format, as long as you give appropriate credit to the original author(s) and the source, provide a link to the Creative Commons license and indicate if changes were made.

The images or other third party material in this chapter are included in the chapter's Creative Commons license, unless indicated otherwise in a credit line to the material. If material is not included in the chapter's Creative Commons license and your intended use is not permitted by statutory regulation or exceeds the permitted use, you will need to obtain permission directly from the copyright holder.

XP 2019 Panel: Agile Manifesto – Impacts on Culture, Education, and Software Practices

Dennis Mancl[1]([⊠]) [iD] and Steven D. Fraser[2] [iD]

[1] MSWX Software Experts, Bridgewater, NJ 08807, USA
dmancl@acm.org
[2] Innoxec, Santa Clara, CA, USA
sdfraser@acm.org

Abstract. Manifestos are often a vehicle to trigger change by catalyzing discussion around a core group of ideas and values – and there is no doubt that the publication of the "Agile Manifesto" in 2001 increased visibility for an emergent breed of lightweight software practices. The panel discussed how the Agile Manifesto has impacted academic and industry software professionals in the areas of culture, education, and software practices.

Keywords: Agile · Agile Manifesto · Software development practices

1 The Agile Manifesto at XP 2019

The Agile Manifesto [1] is the most widely read statement of agile values and principles. At the time it was written (2001), many of the thought leaders in software development practices were already beginning to use lightweight Agile development methods: Scrum, Extreme Programming, Adaptive Software Development, and others. The term Agile was coined to explain the common values behind all of these lightweight approaches. Many Agile instructors and coaches talk about the Agile Manifesto and its values when they deliver introductory agile training.

But today, many who come to university software engineering courses or corporate training courses in Agile development have never heard of the Agile Manifesto. As Agile approaches to business practices are spreading, the Agile Manifesto looks a bit out of date and developer centric. For example, the Manifesto's opening phrase refers to "better ways of developing software" and one of its four declarations is that "working software" is more important than comprehensive documentation.

Is it time to revise the Agile Manifesto? How is the Manifesto received by a new generation of Agile practitioners, and what kind of impact is the Manifesto likely to make on the future of Agile education and Agile culture?

The panel represented both academic and industry experiences. Rebecca Wirfs-Brock is a design methodologist, a consultant on patterns and Agility, and an author of two influential books on software design. Rebecca is the founder of Wirfs-Brock Associates and is based in Oregon. She also serves as the Director of the Agile Experience Reports initiative for the Agile Alliance. Maria Paasivaara is an Associate

© The Author(s) 2019
R. Hoda (Ed.): XP 2019 Workshops, LNBIP 364, pp. 143–148, 2019.
https://doi.org/10.1007/978-3-030-30126-2_17

Professor at IT University of Copenhagen, with experience in running empirical studies in the area of software engineering and software development practices. Werner Wild is an Agile coach and consultant with Evolution Consulting in Austria, and he has significant teaching experience at technical universities in several European countries. Evelyn Tian is a full-stack Agile coach and trainer with Evelyn Konsult AB, based in Sweden. She has coached companies and collaborated with universities on different continents, and she is an Advisor to IEEE Software Board. Steven Fraser, the panel impresario, is based in California where he advises on tech transfer and open innovation strategies for Innoxec. Previously he was the Director of the Cisco Research Center and the Lead for HP's Global University Programs – and he has organized and delivered over 75 software engineering conferences, panels, and workshops.

2   Agile Manifesto Panel Discussion

In this panel session, the panelists explored a number of questions about the Agile Manifesto's impact on culture, process, and education in the software development community. The main discussion topics:

- Is it time to update the Agile Manifesto?
- How has the Manifesto affected the educational practices we use to teach software development in universities?
- How useful are Agile games in education?
- How do we assign grades to students when they are asked to work on a project as part of a team?

Some people believe in the Agile Manifesto with a religious fervor, and they would never want to change it. Other people believe the Agile Manifesto should be "agile," which means it should evolve as needed. And there are some complaints that the Agile Manifesto is too old and too limited, maybe as a result of the biases of a group of 17 specific people in a mindset of 2001 technology – it has been pointed out before that the group was all male persons (no women) and mostly consultants.

The panelists were asked about whether it would be a good idea to update the Agile Manifesto to take into account eighteen years of evolution in Agile development practices as well as the increased interest in applying Agility to non-software problems in business. Rebecca Wirfs-Brock asserted that the Manifesto not likely to change: it is "immutable… at this point in time." Because the Manifesto is owned by the original authors, it will never be changed. Maria Paasivaara agreed, citing a 2018 journal paper by Philipp Hohl and others that summarized some recent interviews with the original Manifesto authors [2].

Even if they can't change the Manifesto, many people who want to be Agile feel compelled to extend it. Rebecca mentioned seeing this compulsion in her role working with Agile experience reports. She has seen a trend for Agile teams to talk about their attempts to "rewrite the Manifesto" to fit different contexts, including projects that don't involve software. She gave an example: "We had someone last year writing about how these principles and practices were restated for working in a research laboratory." In almost every case, their changes are minor edits of the Manifesto text, not major reworking of the content or structure. It is clear that they find that the principles and values of the original Manifesto are "mostly" true, just software focused.

The Agile Manifesto became popular in the 2000s because of "good timing," according to Rebecca. It was written at a time when many researchers and industry managers saw the software industry swinging in the direction of heavyweight software development techniques such as the Rational Unified Process, with formal design diagrams and a complex design lifecycle. But there always was an active software development process counterculture, and the ideas of lightweight process had been explored for many years. It just needed a catalyst to turn into a visible movement.

Rebecca explained that the authors of the Agile Manifesto found a way to stir things up, to rally other people to follow a different path. "Manifestos are like shaking your fist in the air, declaring that this is something different. It was trying to pivot the pendulum from this stodgy, heavy process."

All of the panelists had examples of the impact of Agile on software engineering education. The biggest trend in many universities is to have students work on real-world problems, where they will get direct experience in the Agile mindset. Many educators feel that this is a much better than having their students learn a set of Agile practices merely by reading a book or attending a traditional lecture-based course.

The panel session audience included some faculty members from universities that were still following the model of standard lecture courses. These professors were curious about how they could improve the educational process for their students. Rebecca suggested something simple: "You just announce that you are setting up a practicum with project-based work, and then start doing it in an agile way." A professor could recruit some local small businesses to get involved (to propose some small software development projects) and some students to do the development work (with professors or students acting as Agile coaches). Students will learn a lot from the experience of talking with customers and demonstrating their software to real users.

Werner Wild mentioned his personal experiences with Agile training from his many years of teaching at universities in several European countries. Werner explained the evolution in teaching: "Teaching changed completely from lecturing to walking around. I did a measurement on my last course at TTU in Denmark, we had 70 students spread all over a floor like this here, and I walked between 6 and 10 km every day between the teams." Instead of lecture, Werner's university courses today offer more opportunities for students to work together on real software projects. His role has changed "from hierarchy to face-to-face teaching" and he acts "as more of a coach rather than just presenting the wisdom of previous generations."

Maria and Evelyn explained that companies are often pulled into using Agile by students, and students are finding that companies are looking for interns and new hires with knowledge of Agile.

Maria explained that some companies got interested in Scrum by working with student teams. She recently taught a pilot course where student teams worked on small Agile projects with outside companies. One of the companies was not using Agile, but one person from the company acted as a Product Owner for the student team. "He liked Scrum so much when he saw how the students were working that he decided that they will start using Scrum in their company. Now they are starting to learn Scrum just because of our student team."

Evelyn told the story about markets pushing students to learn Agile. She collaborated with universities at both undergraduate and master level to teach about Agile, Scrum and Product Ownership. "When students were looking for jobs at job fairs, most companies were looking for Agile and Scrum. The university started to feel the pressure, and university folks started to think that we should teach Agile to their students." Evelyn worked closely with universities to help the situation. The goal was to have students equipped with foundation-level knowledge and practices, ready to contribute.

Maria talked about creative education and training approaches in the Agile world. One questioner was interested in hearing more about the value of "Agile games, workshops, and special learning experiences." Maria uses Agile games in many of her university courses, and she has written several conference papers on the subject [3]. In the panel session, Maria recounted her experiences at two universities: "Students really like to use the games. They are really engaged. When I have asked their opinion afterwards, and they say that in the game sessions, the time just flies." She uses games to teach Scrum (using a Scrum Lego game) and Kanban (Test Kanban game).

Werner agreed on the value of games in early Agile training: "Games are one of the things that drew me into field, because it was always fun. You run into things that crazy-looking at first glance, but when you apply it you realize how valuable they are."

Games can play an important role in educating corporate executives about the Agile mindset. Evelyn Tian explained that after running an Agile game, she would get the executives to do an activity to reflect on the Agile Manifesto – to create their own Leadership Manifesto by writing four new statements in the form "we value A over B" for the context of executive management. When she coaches companies who are considering to adopt an Agile scaling framework, she would ask the managers to reflect and create a Scaling Manifesto. The managers would therefore consider the factors behind the scaling practices, rather than just going with a framework that makes them feel safe and then move into pure implementation mode.

Assigning grades to students for project work is a big challenge. One questioner asked: "So much of Agile is about teamwork and collaboration, yet the university insists on individual assessment. How can we motivate students to really get involved in Agile and really play nice in a team, when we are only really assessing them as individuals?"

Everyone shared some experiences about how they assigned grades for team projects. The grading process shouldn't be limited to assigning grades to each code module written. Rebecca noted that the learning process isn't limited to students developing their coding skills: "People pick up skills and contribute in different ways on Agile projects. Not everyone is the fastest coder or algorithm designer, but they can contribute to the team."

One approach to grading is to assign group grades. When Maria was a professor in Finland, she was able to assign grades by team: "In Finland, we worked it so that every member of a team receives the same grade, unless the team members decide they want to give a lower grade to one person who has not contributed that much and then give another person a higher grade." When Maria moved to Denmark, she had to change her approach to grading, because educational regulations in Denmark require instructors to assign individual grades. When Werner was a professor in Copenhagen, he had each team give final project presentations – and there was a fixed set of project questions which they posed to team members in a round-robin sequence. It became very clear when there was a team member who hadn't contributed to the team's final product.

The panelists referred to "Agile mindset" throughout the discussion.

Maria noticed the Agile Manifesto is not a well-known document among the current generation of computer science students. Although most of her students already knew a little bit about Agile when they came to her class, "what they always seem to know is the some of the practices. When I ask them if they know what thoughts underlie the practices – what is says in the Manifesto – they have no idea." She isn't sure how to teach the mindset, but she thinks that the mindset is more important than the practices.

Rebecca and Evelyn both believed that it takes time to teach the Agile mindset, and beginners to Agile may need to get some experience with the practices before their brains can absorb the concepts of the Agile mindset. Rebecca explained "when you are a beginner, you do things without asking why or knowing why." But she also pointed out that some beginners will be curious, and they will ask why. While supporting organizations with Agile transformation, Evelyn said she focuses on encouraged behaviors that are aligned with Agile values and principles, which reduces uncertainties and also builds an environment to experience the values and principles. She explained some of the logic behind experiential learning: "Instead of lecture-based training that tries to convince people that something is important by telling them so, it is better to have them experience the value and get convinced by themselves."

Werner related his experiences teaching Agile concepts to people outside of the software developer community. He has already been successful teaching Agile to management consultants in the Chamber of Commerce in Innsbruck, Austria, and he is looking forward delivering an introductory Agile course to 10-year-olds in Innsbruck in summer 2019.

3 Summary

While the Agile Manifesto will remain unchanged for the foreseeable future, it has already succeeded in creating a revolution in software development practices. Certainly there will be new ways of doing things in the future, so many people will continue to feel the need to write their own version of the Manifesto to apply to their own context. The Manifesto will continue to have an impact on culture, education, and software practices. The panelists focused on Agile's impact on both the content and style of teaching software development – especially in European universities. In Europe, many universities have included Agile development in their curriculum, to meet the demand from industrial companies in Europe. One of the biggest challenges in teaching the practices and values embodied in the Agile Manifesto is how to teach students the Agile mindset.

References

1. Beck, K., Beedle, M., van Bennekum, A., et al.: Manifesto for Agile Software Development (2001). http://agilemanifesto.org. Accessed 19 June 2019
2. Hohl, P., et al.: Back to the future: origins and directions of the "Agile Manifesto" – views of the originators. J. Softw. Eng. Res. Dev. **6**(1) (2018). https://doi.org/10.1186/s40411-018-0059-z
3. Paasivaara, M., Heikkilä, V., Lassenius, C., Toivola, T.: Teaching students scrum using LEGO blocks. In: Companion Proceedings of the 36th International Conference on Software Engineering - ICSE Companion 2014 (2014). https://doi.org/10.1145/2591062.2591169

Open Access This chapter is licensed under the terms of the Creative Commons Attribution 4.0 International License (http://creativecommons.org/licenses/by/4.0/), which permits use, sharing, adaptation, distribution and reproduction in any medium or format, as long as you give appropriate credit to the original author(s) and the source, provide a link to the Creative Commons license and indicate if changes were made.

The images or other third party material in this chapter are included in the chapter's Creative Commons license, unless indicated otherwise in a credit line to the material. If material is not included in the chapter's Creative Commons license and your intended use is not permitted by statutory regulation or exceeds the permitted use, you will need to obtain permission directly from the copyright holder.

XP 2019 Panel: Business Agility

Dennis Mancl[1]([✉]) [iD] and Steven D. Fraser[2] [iD]

[1] MSWX Software Experts, Bridgewater, NJ 08807, USA
dmancl@acm.org
[2] Innoxec, Santa Clara, CA, USA
sdfraser@acm.org

Abstract. Is "Business Agility" the next frontier for Agile? With increased visibility, companies are adopting Agility into the diverse functions of their organizations – moving beyond engineering and IT – to operations, marketing, sales, human resources, and administration. This panel at the XP 2019 conference discussed the latest Agile trend and its implications for practitioners and businesses worldwide.

Keywords: Agile · Business Agility

1 Business Agility at XP 2019

Business Agility is a new and challenging topic for the Agile community and the XP conference. It's a "new market" for Agility, with more consulting and coaching jobs to support business transformations. Although many of the Agile principles are similar, Business Agility is very different from Agile development for software products. Agile coaches and consultants are learning to understand the problems of organizations across the business, and they are discovering how to build seamless interactions between the business and IT.

The panelists shared their views based on their Agile experience and business experience. Two panelists are experienced Agile coaches, and two panelists are directly involved in program management, which requires working with product development teams in engineering or IT as well as other business functions such as sales, finance, and human resources. Steve Adolph is an Agile coach working for cPrime and he is based in Vancouver, Canada. Jutta Eckstein is an independent consultant and coach based in Germany. She is the author of several books on approaches to scaling Agile and using Business Agility practices. Annika Arnholt is a Principal Program Manager at Veritas Technologies based in Minnesota, where she is involved in supporting NetBackup, a complex product that has 50 Scrum teams working across the globe on its development. Nithyanandam Mathiyazhagan (Mathi) is a Lead Program Manager for Strategic Services at John Hancock in Boston, where he manages some of their digital transformation initiatives. Steven Fraser, the panel impresario, is based in California where he advises on tech transfer and open innovation strategies for Innoxec. Previously he was the Director of the Cisco Research Center and the Lead for HP's Global University Programs – and he has organized and delivered over 75 software engineering conferences, panels, and workshops.

© The Author(s) 2019
R. Hoda (Ed.): XP 2019 Workshops, LNBIP 364, pp. 149–153, 2019.
https://doi.org/10.1007/978-3-030-30126-2_18

2 Business Agility Panel Discussion

Business Agility is the application of Agile practices and the Agile mindset beyond the technical community of engineering and IT. The panelists offered two different definitions of the core concepts of Business Agility.

Steve Adolph proposed a definition that is focused on creating a winning business strategy: "Be able to learn faster than your competitor." The practices of Business Agility should be directed at helping the business to introduce new products faster and respond quickly to changes in the marketplace. Steve says that Business Agility aims to "dissolve the artificial barrier between business and IT." The goal is to get seamless interactions across the organization. Business Agility is a competitive strategy to gain market share, reduce costs, or improve the product lifecycle. Steve gave several examples of companies that were able to compete successfully by reducing the time to introduce new products, which allowed them to respond to what their customers wanted.

Steve emphasized the fact that businesses are competing in an Agile world: "You can't be a fast follower anymore." If you just try to play catch up to competitors, you will fall further and further behind.

Jutta Eckstein gave a definition that focused on business flexibility in the face of disruption. Jutta said that Business Agility is a set of techniques to help a business be "more flexible, adaptive, nimble, and responsive – surviving and thriving on disruption." To build an Agile business, the organizational transformation must include decentralized decision-making, improved internal feedback, and improved feedback to and from the customers [1].

Jutta explained that Business Agility doesn't imply always being ahead of the competition. "There are a lot of companies out there who are not ahead of the competitors, and they are doing really well. Not everyone is first. I wouldn't take this as a mark for being agile, or for Business Agility conformance." Jutta said that even if a company isn't the fastest or the best, there is still a lot of value to making the business more flexible and responsive.

Both Steve and Jutta agreed that Business Agility is not directly related to the Agile Manifesto or Scrum. Some of the standard Agile principles are useful, such as teamwork and breaking down silos. But Steve warned against using the IT organization to "drive" a company-wide Business Agility transformation, especially if they take a purely software-centric view of Agility. An agile transformation has to do more than merely teach Scrum to a company's marketing and HR teams. There is a danger that the so-called transformation will just be an excuse for the technical folks to tell finance and HR how to do their jobs.

Both of these definitions are useful. By focusing on competition, Steve's definition is easier to justify to business leaders. The focus of this definition is on continuous learning and improving – which sends a message to everyone that Business Agility transformation is much more than just one day of training. Jutta's definition is useful because it explains some of the key principles of Business Agility, and it is a reminder that centralized decision-making, poor communication, and weak feedback are the trademarks of the old traditional stovepipe organizations.

One questioner asked the key question early in the panel discussion: "Is Business Agility a solution looking for a problem? Should the Agile community be learning from business, rather than the other way around?" Another audience member had a cynical response to the trend towards Business Agility. He claimed that it was mostly a way for Agile experts to sell more tools and consultancy work.

Jutta defended the Business Agility trend, explaining that Business Agility is a reaction to the faster pace of business. "There is a need for becoming faster, more flexible, and more responsive… I think that is what Business Agility does." She agreed that we need to listen other people. "Is it us teaching HR or finance? I don't think it is. However, they see need for Agility as well, and Business Agility is kind of based on the success we're having with Agile." Jutta explained that we can learn from other companies and other fields: "It would be arrogant to say we know it all."

Steve noted that Business Agility is needed because IT is a fundamental constraint for many companies to introduce new products and business processes. Business Agility's goal is to meet real business needs, to make sure that "IT is no longer the constraint on business to compete."

Annika Arnholt pointed out that there are some companies that don't really need to think about Business Agility. On the other hand, she found that in many tech-related companies, Business Agility can build bridges. She has observed that an increased focus on Agile development in engineering and IT will increase the divide between the technical teams and other business organizations – and Business Agility might help restore the relationship. She explained that a company should want to have everyone rowing in the same direction.

One questioner was troubled by the chaos he has seen among the leaders many companies. "When I walk into an organization and meet the CEOs and CFOs, they often have conflicting interests." Each organization tries to maximize their bonuses, without concern for the business as a whole. The question is: "Where's the incentive… unless we change the mindset at the highest level… to even mention Business Agility?"

All of the panelists agreed that "changing the mindset" is essential to success with Business Agility. But teaching and learning the Agile mindset is a big challenge. The discussion about education issues continued throughout the panel session.

Steve pointed out the revolution that has started in education. The best grade schools are less focused on lecture-based learning, and Steve shared a personal story: "The school my daughter goes to is quite fundamentally different from the schools I went to. The students are learning more collaboratively and there are greater opportunities." Collaborative games like Minecraft encourage young people to solve problems together. Steve thinks that "education is a huge frontier for us." It might be the next Agile, especially helping businesses that need continual learning.

One questioner pointed out that most masters-level business students don't know or don't care about Business Agility. How can we inculcate the Agile mindset in students?

Jutta pointed out that if we want to affect the mindset, we should focus on teaching behaviors: "I always struggle with the belief that we can teach mindset or change mindset. What I believe is that we can change behavior, and behavior changes will change our habits, and then a new mindset emerges." The mindset change is the product of getting people to change their habits – to change how they work.

Mathi had some constructive advice for new staff members who are entering companies to start their career:

- Try to integrate into the organization ("fake it until you make it").
- When you see that change is needed, work to create a strong peer network. This kind of social support can create consensus to change the way things are being done.
- Include feedback in the process: come up with your own targets, metrics that help you "define your own success."

Mathi emphasized the idea that learning in the business context may come from different directions: "Our mission is to learn, and learning comes in various shapes. We might learn from the competition. Also, fresh voices coming into the organization could be a source of learning."

The panelists pointed to the value of decentralized decision-making to support Business Agility. Annika talked about decentralization as a fundamental idea in Business Agility. Teams need to be empowered to make decisions themselves. Jutta thought that when leadership tries to centralize decisions, it can be an indicator that the company's leadership doesn't understand the need for Business Agility. It can also make the organization way too slow. Jutta explained that an ideal Agile organization would "use the innovative potential of every employee, without waiting for a think tank or design thinking session because this will be too slow."

The panel was asked about the Agility (or lack of Agility) in the design of products. The questioner complained that many products become way too complicated over time – a company responds to customer requests by adding new functionality, but they never take anything away or rethink the tangled structure.

Mathi agreed with the questioner. Rather than adding features endlessly, Mathi advocated simplifying a product so it can be better understood by a direct consumer. "Simplicity is the name of the game, not adding more things on top of what is already there." Steve explained that many companies have complex products because they have a design culture that is obsessed with overengineering, because they believe that "digital is best." Every product seems to be loaded up with many unnecessary digital features. Business Agility should include the concept of keeping the products simple.

A final question addressed Business Agility for non-profit organizations. "We have been working on Business Agility with civic councils, charities, and universities, not in the commercial world. A charity is not trying to be ahead of business or competition, it is just trying to survive and do the right thing or positive things in the world."

Jutta agreed that competition and profit may not be an organization's primary goal. A company, government, or non-profit may be interested in other issues, such as sustainability. "Maybe a company will only stay in business if it looks after the environment and is seen by the public as environmentally friendly."

Annika was concerned about potential negative effects of always talking about "competition" when introducing Business Agility. "I hear people say they are uncomfortable with the competitive mindset." She accepted that we need to think about our competitors, but a primary focus (and measurement of success) that concentrates on "crushing" the competition may be unhealthy and promote behaviors that are inconsistent with an Agile mindset. Our primary focus should be on what is right for the customer and our organization.

In their concluding comments, the panelists supported the goals of Business Agility. Jutta claimed that Business Agility is "beyond Agile – it is about having a holistic view on the company," but the teams need to buy into the purpose of Business Agility. Annika explained the importance of cross-team collaboration – that the teams need to see themselves as "not one big warship but a fleet of speedboats, all rowing in the same direction." Mathi thought that Business Agility must "span into corporate social responsibility and into the entire business ecosystem." Steve emphasized the importance of learning: "We're going to have to rename this conference from XP to XL – for Extreme Learning."

3 Summary

Business Agility is a set of business practices that go beyond introducing Agility into software development. An Agile business organizes itself to introduce new products faster and respond quickly to changes in the marketplace. The business decentralizes decision-making, improves communication, and improves internal feedback and feedback from customers. If decision-making is still centralized and there is weak communication and feedback across the enterprise, then the business is going to be too slow to react to change.

All of the panelists warned that Business Agility is not directly related to the Agile Manifesto or Scrum. One way it may fail is if technical folks assume Business Agility gives them the authority to tell finance and HR how to do their jobs.

Teaching and learning the Agile mindset is not easy – and the panel believed that a new mindset emerges from changes in behavior and habits. There are multiple sources of learning: learning from coworkers, learning from the competition, and learning from fresh voices coming into the organization. Business Agility will continue to evolve, but it is not a destination or a checkbox.

Reference

1. Eckstein, J., Buck, J.: Company-Wide Agility with Beyond Budgeting, Open Space & Sociocracy. CreateSpace Independent Publishing Platform, Scotts Valley (2018)

Open Access This chapter is licensed under the terms of the Creative Commons Attribution 4.0 International License (http://creativecommons.org/licenses/by/4.0/), which permits use, sharing, adaptation, distribution and reproduction in any medium or format, as long as you give appropriate credit to the original author(s) and the source, provide a link to the Creative Commons license and indicate if changes were made.

The images or other third party material in this chapter are included in the chapter's Creative Commons license, unless indicated otherwise in a credit line to the material. If material is not included in the chapter's Creative Commons license and your intended use is not permitted by statutory regulation or exceeds the permitted use, you will need to obtain permission directly from the copyright holder.

XP 2019 Panel: Agile, the Next 20 Years

Dennis Mancl[1]([⊠]) [iD] and Steven D. Fraser[2] [iD]

[1] MSWX Software Experts, Bridgewater, NJ 08807, USA
dmancl@acm.org
[2] Innoxec, Santa Clara, CA, USA
sdfraser@acm.org

Abstract. A panel of university staff and industry Agile experts were invited to conclude the XP 2019 conference with a discussion of the conference theme: "Agile – the Next 20 Years: Share and Discover!" The panelists gave their views of the value of the Agile Manifesto, the possible future of Agile scaling frameworks, and some ideas for improving industry-university collaboration.

Keywords: Agile · Design

1 The Next 20 Years in Agile

The first XP conference was held in 2000 in Cagliari, Italy – and that conference attracted many software practitioners who were excited about lightweight and iterative development methods like Extreme Programming. Today, at the twentieth XP conference, there is still a lot of interest and excitement about Agile among practitioners and researchers. Twenty years from now, will there still be the same level of enthusiasm for Agile software development? Maybe everything will be called Agile. Maybe all large software product development projects will use a single standard Agile scaling framework similar to one of the approaches being used today. Or maybe today's Agile practices will have evolved into new and better development methods.

The members of the panel came from all corners of the world and all parts of the Agile community. Deepti Jain is an Agile practitioner and coach, and she is the founder of AgileVirgin, based in India. Nils Brede Moe is a research manager at SINTEF in Norway and a researcher at Blekinge Institute of Technology. Helen Sharp is a professor at The Open University in the United Kingdom, and her research interests include human and social aspects of software development. Ken Power is an independent consultant based in Ireland. Philippe Kruchten is a professor of software engineering at the University of British Columbia, in Vancouver, Canada. Steven Fraser, the panel impresario, is based in California where he advises on tech transfer and open innovation strategies for Innoxec. Previously he was the Director of the Cisco Research Center and the Lead for HP's Global University Programs – and he has organized and delivered over 75 software engineering conferences, panels, and workshops. Philippe and Steve served as the Program Co-chairs for XP 2019.

© The Author(s) 2019
R. Hoda (Ed.): XP 2019 Workshops, LNBIP 364, pp. 154–158, 2019.
https://doi.org/10.1007/978-3-030-30126-2_19

The majority of the panelists agreed that Agile will be around 20 years from now, in some form:

- Helen Sharp: "Agile will be around for quite a while to come yet. In 20 years, we may not be calling it that, but it will still be here."
- Deepti Jain: "I think that in 20 years, we will be working more independently. We will look forward to creating something that works best for us."
- Nils Brede Moe: "I have been doing research in Agile for the last 15 years. I've seen many different companies and many different cultures. It's being practiced differently, and I think for the next 20 years, it will still be practiced differently."
- Ken Power: "In terms of the next 20 years – I have no idea… I'm optimistic we will see a lot of interesting things in the next 20 years."
- Philippe Kruchten: "Agile is there forever. It's not going to be replaced. Maybe the adjective 'Agile' will diminish a little bit. But the mindset behind Agile, which is to constantly observe your environment and react or respond to it as fast as possible, that's going to be there forever."

2   The Next 20 Years Panel Discussion

At the end of a long and exhausting week, this panel still had the energy to discuss many interesting topics. Most of them agreed that Agile will be around in some form 20 years from now, but it might have a different name in the future. The panelists explained that the Agile Manifesto will have diminishing value to the Agile community over time. The panelists offered their opinions about the future of Agile scaling frameworks and related tools. They complained that the frameworks add too much complexity, and they also limit the ability of teams to tailor their way of working. Another important discussion was about how to increase the collaboration and communication between researchers and practitioners.

In their introductions, the panelists each presented their favorite issues relating to Agile methods in the future. Deepti Jain explained that 20 years from now, developers will be working more independently. Some of the current Agile frameworks will be too constraining: "Many folks will not want to be attached to an organization, or a framework or a structure." Nils Brede Moe believed that there will be many useful applications for today's research work on autonomous teams. But Nils saw technology transfer as a major issue: "As researchers, we need to be better at bridging research and practice." Helen Sharp was sure that there is a future for Agile methods: "Agile was here before we called it Agile. And Agile will be here 20 years from now whether we call it agile or we call it something else." Ken Power complained that he has no idea where things will be in 20 years, but he had advice for the near future. He claimed that the real innovators in Agile work will not waste their time arguing about labels. They will be exploring the interactions of Agile with other computing technologies: maybe flow-based development, maybe artificial intelligence and machine learning.

Philippe Kruchten injected a bit of humor into his introduction – but his serious point was that there will be a swinging pendulum of support for Agile. In the short term, he thought that the likeliest reaction to Agile will be popular obsession in the practitioner community. ("All business functions will become Agile: Agile accounting, Agile marketing, Agile kindergarten. SAFe becomes an ISO standard, Scrum is taught in grade 3.") But in 10 years or so, this obsession may be followed by a revolution rejecting Agile.

Philippe also offered a list of interesting technology work in Agile, enough to keep researchers busy for 20 years. We have to learn to avoid a "one size fits all" process. We think we know what coordination, communication, and collaboration are – "but when you dig a little bit, you realize it is extremely different across the spectrum of the field into which we apply Agile." We need to learn more about project governance and the concept of value.

There was a question about the future of the Agile Manifesto. "Is it a document that gets revered and a religion emerges around it? Or is it sent to the dustbin of history?" Helen asked "Shouldn't it evolve? Shouldn't it be Agile and be changed as time goes on?" Steve Fraser, the panel impresario, recalled the conclusions of the Agile Manifesto panel from earlier in the week. That panel had agreed that the Manifesto is not going to be changed. There had been a discussion about the origins of Agile and the significance of the Manifesto: "There was the observation that Agile existed before the Manifesto. But the Manifesto was seen as a defining moment, and it did both good and perhaps had some negative influence on the culture of the community." Philippe looked to the future: "I think the Manifesto has served its purpose. We should stop referring to it. We know the flaws that it contains, and we should just move on. You cannot define that your organization is Agile by compliance with the Manifesto."

Helen and Philippe were skeptical about claims that we will have robots doing all of the coding work in the next 20 years. Helen pointed to similar forecasts made 35 years ago, when "expert systems" were supposed to put programmers out of work. She thinks that "software development will change, but I don't think it will change in that way... I don't think it's going to be automatic." Philippe explained that AI and Machine Learning may bring some new tools to support programmers, such as tools to help them navigate large and complex code bases. But automated tools won't be able to create new designs. "The real decisions about design, I don't think they can be automated."

Ken also hoped for technology to give us better programming tools. "The bottleneck in software development is not the interface between the developer and the keyboard and the computer. The bottleneck, especially as systems get larger, is learning and creating shared understanding. I think we'll see a lot of innovation improving learning and tools to help with shared understanding. I think that's where the innovation will be over the next 20 years."

One questioner (Maria Paasivaara from IT-University Copenhagen and XP 2020 General Chair) asked about Agile scaling frameworks: "What is the future regarding scaling frameworks? Are we going to have all companies using some of the scaling frameworks? Or will they disappear?"

At the beginning of the XP 2019 conference, Scott Ambler had delivered a provocative keynote talk titled "#NoFrameworks: How We Can Take Agile Back!" [1]. In that talk, Scott explained that Agile teams should be allowed to choose their own way of working. But the current Agile scaling frameworks are simplistic solutions, promising great results after a few days of certification training.

Helen offered one benefit of Agile scaling frameworks: they help individuals structure their work. "The thing about frameworks is that they help you understand what kinds of things need to be done, and it gives you vocabulary and context that allow people to work." But she pointed out that there is a danger of trying to solve all problems with the same cookie cutter.

Nils didn't like the extra complexity that results from using the scaling frameworks. "You will see the frameworks for long time, because many people are making a lot of money out of them. But some people will raise questions. The frameworks are making things more complicated and more complex." We need to make companies and projects less complex in the future to handle external complexity. Instead of simple jobs in complex organizations we need complex jobs in simple organizations. Nils thought that how to "scale up" Agile development is the wrong question: "People are asking how to scale, while research shows that companies are making things more and more complex, so the question for the future may be how to scale things down."

Deepti added that "it's about systems thinking." She said that it can take genera-tions to make a shift in how we think. She also explained that companies are reluctant to build their own framework. It is hard to spend the time to explore, unlearn, and relearn. "No one has time or energy for that. So they will go for the framework from the external expert or consultant."

Philippe thinks that the frameworks will fade away. He recalled the object oriented wars in the 1990s, which was a competition between several major object oriented design methods that each had its own standard diagrams. (Philippe paused and added: "I still miss the little clouds of the Booch notation.") But although today's generation of soft-ware developers uses popular object oriented languages like Java and Python, they don't use the diagrams. The same thing may happen to Agile scaling frameworks. "I think at some point in time, after some battles, some conferences, and a competition to be the first one to be an ISO standard, they will disappear, perhaps about 15 years from now."

Other questioners explored the future opportunities for collaboration between companies and universities. "This conference has been a meeting place between prac-titioners and researchers. If you are a company seeking advice on development methods, you get most of the advice from practitioners or consulting companies. In the next 20 years, do you see anything researchers can do to get involved more involved in practice?"

Philippe explained that improving access to research publications can be a big help. He noted that the XP conference has started publishing its proceedings as Open Access. "Most independent developers, like my son here in Montreal, don't have access to IEEE Xplore and ACM Digital Library." (An individual subscription to ACM Digital Library or IEEE Xplore is relatively expensive.) Philippe also thought that consortia - groups of software companies who team up with academia - are a good forum to increase the interactions between researchers and practitioners. He praised the Scandinavian governments who have provided funding for long-term consortia.

Ken addressed this question from the practitioner viewpoint: "We practitioners have a responsibility to innovate and disseminate the results of our industry innovation through various channels." But he challenged university researchers to do a better job of collaboration with industry: "There is an opportunity to treat practitioners not as research subjects but as research partners – to engage more in a partnership model. Co-author papers, co-lead studies – Agile research has a lot of promise for industry-academic collaboration."

Nils agreed that collaborative work is good, but we may need to change the way we publish research work to make it more useful to practitioners. "Maybe we need to change the way we communicate our results – in a way that make more sense for practitioners, so we can have a better dialog between researchers and practitioners. Unfortunately, researchers just talk to researchers and practitioners to practitioners." Philippe liked the idea and added his own suggestions: "Maybe we need also other kinds of publications than the relatively rigid style that we use in Journal of Systems and Software and Springer-Verlag journals. The industry people would like to read what we write, but maybe we need to make things a little bit more approachable. We could have the rigorous things, with all the evidence, research questions, and threat to validity, and then we write another simplified version with a little more guidance for the practitioners to work with and give us feedback."

3   Summary

The panel members' crystal balls might be a bit cloudy, but they are mostly optimistic about the future of Agile. Agile will be around in some form 20 years from now, although it may have a different name, but software development organizations will still need strong team collaboration and the ability to respond to change. It is unlikely that AI and Machine Learning will replace programmers, but new AI-based programming tools would be welcome. The demand for Agile scaling frameworks will grow for a while, but they will probably fade away over time. Researchers and practitioners will still need to communicate and share ideas: experimental results, empirical studies, new ideas for Agile practices, and new ways of teaching and learning about the Agile mindset.

Reference

1. Ambler, S.: #NoFrameworks: How We Can Take Agile Back (2019). http://disciplinedagil edelivery.com/noframeworks-xp2019/. Accessed 20 June 2019

Open Access This chapter is licensed under the terms of the Creative Commons Attribution 4.0 International License (http://creativecommons.org/licenses/by/4.0/), which permits use, sharing, adaptation, distribution and reproduction in any medium or format, as long as you give appropriate credit to the original author(s) and the source, provide a link to the Creative Commons license and indicate if changes were made.

The images or other third party material in this chapter are included in the chapter's Creative Commons license, unless indicated otherwise in a credit line to the material. If material is not included in the chapter's Creative Commons license and your intended use is not permitted by statutory regulation or exceeds the permitted use, you will need to obtain permission directly from the copyright holder.

Author Index

Printed in the United States
By Bookmasters

Printed in the United States
By Bookmasters